"We hold these truths to be self-evident,
that all men, women, and children, no
matter their race, ethnicity, faith, or sexual
orientation, are ALL created equal, that
they are endowed by their Creator with
certain unalienable Rights that among these
are Life, Liberty, the Pursuit of Happiness,
and To Live in Peace with one another."

Which do you prefer, this version or the original?

THE
NEGLECTED
MINORITY

DO MEXICANS MATTER?

Federico Maese, MD

For my mother, Dr. Martha Sánchez-Craig, and my uncles Javier Sánchez Aguirre and Armando Fuentes Aguirre (aka Catón), all passionate narrators of Mexican history and possessors of that unique Mexican sense of picaresque humor that perhaps contributes to the so-called Hispanic Paradox.

TABLE OF CONTENTS

INTRODUCTION

Some thirty years ago my grandfather questioned me on the wisdom

of accepting a training position in Internal Medicine at the prestigious Baylor College of Medicine program in Houston, Texas. At the time he was in semi-retirement from a long career as an Agricultural Engineer in Mexico. He had served first as a Dean of the Antonio Narro School of Agriculture in Saltillo, Mexico, a quaint colonial city renowned worldwide for its artistic clay and ceramic tiles, then he moved on to the PRI's Secretary of Agriculture Department with the important mission of improving Mexico's dairy cattle industry. The story of how my self-starter grandfather arrived in Mexico City has become family lore. I'll spare you, the reader, the unique and comical details, but I will say they are at the core of his comment to me about moving to the United States for medical training.

In his mind, Mexico was simply the best place in the world. He held this belief not because of a lack of traveling outside of Mexico. Quite the contrary, he had studied at Texas A&M University during the Great Depression and travelled the world throughout his life. Yet he always returned home and had professionally flourished in Mexico, with each of his six children obtaining higher education.

He insisted I'd enjoy a plethora of opportunities if I, at the time single and without children, launched a medical practice somewhere along the Mayan Riviera. I replied that although I had just graduated from medical school, I felt that I had limited knowledge and needed top-notch residency training. I suppose he was from an era where a medical graduate would just set up a practice without specialty training. After all, Mexican medical schools are seven years long and include a year of social service, providing along that journey far more hands-on training than U.S. schools.

But his bias about staying in Mexico had a deeper message. He resisted the brain drain phenomenon that had already been occurring when talented Mexican and other Hispanic professionals ended up migrating and staying in the U.S. and other so-called first world countries (a term I personally despise) instead of remaining or returning to their native country to make a difference. Then he paused for a few seconds. In his words there was something else as well. He shared that some intellectuals would describe the historic relationship between Mexico and the U.S., since 1810, as an asymmetric power struggle littered with multiple acts of one-sided aggression.

My Uncle Caton, a well-known writer and historian in Mexico, describes U.S. involvement in Mexican history across the last two centuries as "the inevitable dark thread of Mexican history." My grandfather point blank asked me, "Are you aware of what the U.S. has done to Mexico and how they treat Mexicans?" He told me that when he attended college in Texas, he came across a restaurant sign that said, "We don't serve dogs, Blacks, or Mexicans." I ignorantly replied that I didn't know about any of that. My goal was to get into one of the best specialty training programs in the world and that was somewhere in the U.S. Finally, he told me he understood, but still insisted that I needed to come back to Mexico.

More than 30 years have passed since that conversation. Having lived in the U.S. all this time, I have had a different experience than my grandfather's back in the Texas of the 1930's. I arrived in the U.S. at the end of the Cold War, marked by the 1989 tearing down of the Berlin Wall and subsequent free elections ousting Communist regimes, and culminating in the 1991 dissolution of the Soviet Union. The U.S. clearly stood alone as the most powerful nation on earth. Beyond military and economic prowess, the U.S. seemed to provide millions of people, including minorities and immigrants, the opportunity for prosperity and a chance at the "American Dream." It appeared to me that the overt societal racism of the past, including institutional racism, was difficult to find, except perhaps for isolated pockets. The U.S. as a whole seemed to have made further progress on the accomplishments of the 1960's civil rights movement, gradually embracing and incorporating the ideals put forth some 200 years before by the founding fathers in the Declaration of Independence.

> Overt societal racism of the past, including institutional racism, is difficult to find, except perhaps for isolated pockets.

Training in Houston, Texas, for six and a half years in some of the largest hospitals in the U.S., both public and private, surrounded by people from all over the world, I did not see any evidence of racism or discrimination. Having cared for patients of all ethnicities with the dreaded HIV disease at the height of the epidemic, mostly at Ben Taub Hospital, I experienced with my colleagues, attending physicians, nurses, and technicians the absolute caring dedication to each patient, no matter their race, ethnicity, gender, or sexual orientation, which has remained with me to this day.

After my training I started my first clinic in East Texas, a place that in years past had been a hotbed of open racism and discrimination, especially against Blacks and Mexicans. At the time I was married and my ex-wife, who is half Chinese, was concerned about how we would be treated by the predominantly Baptist, white community. With my degrees in hand and not much in savings, I walked into a branch of Guarantee Bank in Mount Pleasant, Texas, and in a few days had a loan for a brand-new home located by the prestigious country club. Within a few months I obtained a loan for a new clinic property. Then soon enough I received a call at the clinic from Bo Pilgrim, owner of Pilgrim's Pride Chicken located in close-by Pittsburgh, Texas. He invited me for lunch at the country club in Mount Pleasant to discuss his family history of heart disease, his cardiac risk, and the new egg he was promoting with a high vitamin E content. Mr. Pilgrim inquired how I came to set up a cardiology practice in East Texas. I informed him that the famous Texas tobacco attorney, Mr. Harold Nix in Dangerfield, Texas, a Mexican-American War amateur historian, had helped me with a visa matter that required three years of service in a medically underserved community. Mr. Nix and had I enjoyed several social meetings in his home office, full of artifacts from the Mexican-American War that ended in 1848, where I learned much about my own history.

In short time many of the 5000 Mexican employees at Pilgrim's Pride Chicken would become my patients. Of tremendous help was the once a week 16-page newspaper I started with a local Mexican radio personality to highlight news from Mexico. Each Thursday at the Mt. Pleasant Walmart, *La Tribuna de Mt. Pleasant* could be obtained for free. Additionally, during my early days of practice as I was served a hearty enchilada at Two Senoritas restaurant with my family, an elderly woman at an adjacent table suddenly collapsed.

She had that look most cardiologists and emergency room physicians recognize. It wasn't even a choice to leave my piping hot enchiladas unattended to perform CPR on the unfortunate lady in front a full restaurant that continued to enjoy their meals without missing a bite until the ambulance arrived. As it turns out, the lady had a heart attack, complicated by rupturing the tethering chords on her mitral valve, resulting in acute heart failure and a cardiac arrest. She had emergency surgery by an excellent cardiac surgeon and surgical team in a Longview, Texas, hospital. As a physician, I responded according to instinct. I had no idea this event would impact my life beyond that dinner.

Sometime later, a patient came into my new office with a newspaper article describing the incident and the fact that this prominent lady in the East Texas community had survived. Suddenly, my office was flooded with people from all over East Texas wanting to become my patients. It sure didn't feel like anyone cared that I was Mexican.

My Sundays were spent attending the local Baptist church and enjoying brunch with new friends in the community and their families. My children were readily accepted and invited to birthdays and other social events. My entire experience in East Texas from a social standpoint, in spite of the historical warnings, was free of racial issues. I understand some may comment that as an educated individual, medically trained and fully capable of improving the lives of others, one is more likely to be treated with welcoming arms and without discrimination. Perhaps so, but it is genuinely what I experienced.

People may ask, however, about what other Mexicans have experienced in the U.S. What about those who did not have the opportunities that I had? Was my experience unique or an anomaly? Having had degrees prior to arriving in the U.S. plus training at Baylor College of Medicine under prominent world-renowned doctors in multiple medical fields and cardiovascular medicine does provide its advantages, no doubt.

What about the history of Mexicans in the U.S.? What about Mexicans today? As the subtitle of this book asks: Do Mexicans matter?

Of course, to me as a Mexican American, they do. But what about to the national conversation, politics, and policies? It seems that today most of the daily national dialogue is a Black-White binary, with the mainstream media (MSM) mainly focusing on either a "social justice" agenda about white police brutality and racial inequities against Blacks, or the successful razor-sharp mission that contributed to ousting President Trump from office, while elevating President Biden to sainthood.

In 2020, arguably the first year of the novel coronavirus worldwide pandemic and reignited widespread racial protests across the U.S., fear and hate were the predominant concepts portrayed daily by a media intent on dividing the country even further along black and white racial lines.

What about the Mexicans and other Latinos? Are most of these people largely neglected? And if so, why? Is it that Latinos are expected to fulfill their role as an underclass of mute manual laborers, and are thus barely an afterthought in the national discourse? It would appear that politicians and our national media have recently thrown a patronizing morsel of "woke" leftovers to this "Brown" minority, shoved at the last minute into the cramped waste basket known as "people of color." It seems every election cycle we see the usual empty pandering from the political parties on full display.

So, what do we Latinos do? Do we fall for the usual rhetoric and simply vote for those politicians who promise us free stuff and some crooked pathway to equality or, as is the choice word of the day, equity? Instead, we don't put more faith in such promises as we continue to do what we do best: quietly take on back-breaking work and take care of our families. I must ask if that's the right response. Is it time for a change in the U.S. Latino population?

National neglect is evident. Latinos are presently some 18% of the total U.S. population, with those of Mexican descent counting close to 40 million out of the almost 60 million Hispanics. The total African American population stands at about 13%, or about 43 million. Despite the significantly larger population, we Latinos, compared to the Black community, seem to be largely ignored and neglected from the national dialogue. When we are the subjects of a media article or a network news show, it is usually not due to some cultural uplifting matter or personal achievement, but about criminality, illegal immigration, drug trafficking, or some tragedy.

Case in point is the massacre in El Paso in 2019. Can anyone imagine what would have happened across the U.S. if more than twenty Black individuals had been shot and killed and another twenty plus injured at a mall in Detroit by a deranged white supremacist? This clearly was not a police brutality incident, but can anyone say that in 2020 it would not have resulted in a national protest, possibly deteriorating into massive widespread violence? Instead, chances are you haven't even heard of this massacre.

For one day, on August 3, 2019, El Paso, Texas, occupied the national attention. Immediately, most politicians condemned the horrific atrocity, blaming it on a variety of factors that barely scratched the surface of a longstanding historic reality. A massacre of brown-skinned Mexicans had occurred at a local Wal-Mart. The mainstream media reported that a 21-year-old white man with a known white supremacist genocidal agenda from Allen, Texas, had driven some eleven hours to discharge his weapon, killing twenty-two people and wounding twenty-three others of Mexican descent. Most of them were U.S. citizens. Eight victims were Mexican citizens and one German. The massacre was labeled as the worst in history targeting Mexicans. Others outside MSM, such as David Dorado Romo, in his detailed historical Observer article published on August

9, 2019, focused on the long history of anti-Mexican violence at the border, calling it a "deadly epidemic." He pointed to the history entrenched in the mindset of white supremacists who have felt the need to protect America from the "cultural and ethnic replacement" brought on by "the Hispanic invasion of Texas." Mr. Dorado Romo's words chillingly hang in the air as he further highlights the killer's manifesto that stated in no uncertain terms that even though migrants do the dirty work, it is their kids that want to live the "American Dream" by obtaining college degrees and higher paying occupations. The threat is clear. These Mexicans are destroying the racial purity of white America!

But is this new? Is this the worst massacre committed against Mexican individuals in the U.S.? In his article, Mr. Dorado Romo takes the reader on the eye-opening and shocking history of border violence against Mexicans since the early 20th century, when clear-cut institutional racism purposefully employed a variety of tactics to eliminate the "undesirable aliens" deemed genetically inferior. These included immigration restrictions dependent on desirable racial traits, unjust targeted incarceration, forceful deportations of citizens, miscegenation, and literacy immigration laws, as well as racist government sponsored and run sterilization programs. According to Mr. Dorado Romo, a generation of influential racial hygienists, such as Madison Grant, believed that the "Mexican Indian has no racial qualities to contribute to the United States population that are now needed," and recommended that "Mexicans should be deported as fast as they can be located" by any and all means. The author continues to describe the delousing techniques employed at the Santa

Fe International Bridge at the El Paso-Juarez border with toxic chemicals to "cleanse" Mexican crossers during the years surrounding WWI. Among those used was the notorious Zyklon B gas that, on the direct recommendation of Dr. Gerhard Peters in 1937 and inspired by the prior El Paso-Juarez border crossing example, would eventually be employed during World War II by the Nazi Germans to exterminate millions of people deemed as subhuman pests. According to records examined by few, Mexicans were targeted along with African Americans and Native Americans by the eugenicist ideology so prevalent among Caucasian northeastern elites.

From the mid-1800s, after the 1848 Treaty of Guadalupe Hidalgo, and through the 1920s, the famed Texas Rangers, together with multiple vigilante Anglo mobs, exerted control over the southern Texas border with brutal efficiency. Their tactics resulted in the murder of thousands of Mexicans and often included death without a trial by lynching or being shot at point-blank range for the unforgivable sin of being Mexican. With the 2018 one-hundred-year anniversary of the Porvenir Massacre (when fifteen men and boys were shot by Texas Rangers on suspicion – without evidence – of being involved in area thefts and murders), some information has begun to leak out about these racially motivated tragedies.

When one is aware of the dark and horrific events that historically occurred too often around the Mexican-American border, it is easier to understand the reaction to the pictures which came out of the border agents on horses wielding whips. However, this serves as an example of a non-event being used to propagate a certain narrative. Those particular border agents didn't hurt anyone or break any ethical or moral standards, yet they were demonized by the MSM and the current presidential administration. I argue that we should acknowledge the tragedies and rampant racism of the past and their impacts, but not overlay those incidents and motives on people today who don't fit the bill.

The 2019 El Paso massacre is as personal a matter for me as it is for Mr. Dorado Romo, who lost one of his friends from school in the tragedy. The 700,000 people living in El Paso are a tight American community. Some had a family member who was killed or injured, and thousands were friends with or knew some of the victims. I was born in that part of the country and currently have many relatives living in El Paso and Ciudad Juarez, twin city on the Mexican side. My family has been in that region of the country and all the way up to Albuquerque, Santa Fe, and in the Town of Las Vegas in New Mexico since the 1600s. Yes, my relatives on my father's side have lived in those territories since they were part of New Spain, ruled by the Spanish Crown, and subsequently becoming part of Mexico in 1821 after gaining its independence from Spain. So, yes, it's personal. But such a tragedy shouldn't matter to just those to whom it's personal. That's not how the nation reacts to a host of other tragedies, even ones with much less loss of precious life.

In El Paso and Ciudad Juarez, many families are still in shock over the horrific tragedy. Yet, there was no nationwide outcry or rioting in the streets. Can anyone recall a time or incident when an unhinged Mexican, unhappy about the outcome of the Mexican-American War or some other anti-Mexican incident, took it upon himself to target and murder whites at random after writing a manifesto outlining the racial impurity and perdition whites bring and warning them to get "out of our country?" If you are white in the U.S., please do not proclaim you are still in fear of Pancho Villa!

The fact is, the El Paso murders were carried out by a young psychiatrically deranged white supremacist with a history of dangerous behaviors which were mostly ignored by the local authorities. Unfortunately, in the U.S., there are small pockets of such hate groups that we as nation need to identify and do our best to prevent from perpetrating such criminal activities as occurred in El Paso.

Despite such incidents and after living in this country for 30 years, I do not believe racism in any form is a major problem in U.S. society. Instead, I ask: Is it possible to fully recognize that today the overwhelming majority of people, and I truly mean the vast majority of people currently living in the U.S., are NOT racist, do not harbor any prejudice or discrimination against any minority, and would never take a single step, intentionally or unintentionally, to harm in any fashion — physically or emotionally — a person of Mexican descent or other Latinos or African Americans or other minorities?

Let me reiterate. I'm not saying that racism and prejudice don't exist anywhere in the U.S. That would be a ridiculous statement. Racism and prejudice have and do and will always exist in some form or another in all places humans live. What I'm espousing is that America has made tremendous progress in these areas and has successfully rooted out racism and discrimination in the vast majority of the country. But I also fully understand that work remains to be done.

You may not agree with me, but as a first generation Mexican

American, I sincerely believe this is the case. I can only speak from my own experiences, but recognize others may have had different experiences than me and sincerely respect your opinions on this matter if they are different. I have been welcomed and accepted as an equal member in this truly beautiful, amazing, and diverse society that constitutes the United States. In my younger years I lived for prolonged periods in both Mexico and Canada, two nations I hold dear in my heart for all of their own unique cultural traits, history, and, most importantly, on account of all the loving, lifelong friends of mine that live in these two beautiful countries, each with its own identity firmly imprinted in my mind and soul. I have been truly blessed to be a complete North American! Perhaps that is where my perspective originates, from these three countries embracing diverse cultures within them, more alike than different, far friendlier to each other than adversarial, more tolerant in accepting the inevitable unique tapestry of diversity, all necessary components in order to live in respectful harmony in the U.S.

You may ask if in all these years in the U.S. I have ever encountered any form of racism or discrimination. My simple answer is NO. To be honest, over the years there have been three or four minor incidents when someone with a silly, transparent agenda called me a variety of anti-Mexican slurs to my face that I shall not repeat here. I chose not to react and to instead forgive these individuals in my heart and mind for what I prefer to call simple ignorance, possibly poor self-esteem, and maybe even jealousy. It is empowering not to react, not to give credence to such slights as many have done throughout history.

Some might say, "You've experienced racism. You just described it. You simply refuse to see or acknowledge it." But doesn't everyone have negative, ignorant interactions in their lives? The important thing isn't that someone said something stupid or hurtful. It's how we react and respond to what's done and said to us.

It has occurred to me a simple question. What if they truly knew me? Would they feel the same? Just for the record, I do not consider myself a victim. Nor do I believe that today a victimhood mentality, manufactured oppression, or race-based, intersectional, made-up discrimination of any type is helpful to Latinos in the U.S. I believe we are all Americans first and foremost, period! Whatever your ethnicity and racial make-up, you are beautiful and should celebrate your uniqueness. I certainly do and try to teach my children the same. I'd love to see everyone embrace how they were created, with all their individual talents, gifts, knowledge, culture, and ethnic heritage. Even skin color.

When someone who does not know me asks where I'm from, my exuberant reply invariably is, "Where the beautiful people are from!"

Then that person usually replies, "Where is that"?

"I'm from Mexico, Canada and from here, the United States. That's where I'm from!"

In an instant, one can detect more than a smile on the person inquiring. I often see a subtle yet uncontrollable bubbling up of happiness from inside their heart, and an acknowledgement of incontestable truth, for I usually state it with such smiling confidence, especially when these questions and answers are all said in a melodic Spanish that bathes and pleases the senses. Close your eyes for a few seconds and just imagine hearing someone say how much they love where they are from. It can be exhilarating. These are truly the small, yet wonderful, moments in life: to feel great about where one is from, one's ancestry, where one has lived, and where one now considers home. I don't understand people getting offended at being asked where they're from. I love sharing and celebrating my diverse background and heritage. These questions open up doors to unique conversations and learning for all involved.

So, no, I have not experienced racism in the U.S. I am not a victim. I have not been discriminated against, and I am not oppressed. I am a free person, having lived in such countries that legally provide personal guarantees of freedom, protection, and equal opportunity, as well as requiring unique personal responsibilities that each of us must uphold to maintain such precious privileges. All of those who currently enjoy these rights should celebrate and hold them in the highest esteem, close to their heart, for our predecessors gave their lives so we could have them.

Undeniably, as a matter of historical record, there was a time in this nation when these rights were not only denied, but extreme racism, unjust prejudice, and discrimination prevailed against most minorities, especially African Americans, Native Americans, Asians, and Mexicans, as we shall learn in the narrative that follows. It is now my firm belief, even in the aftermath of the tragic El Paso massacre, that such acts of racist terrorism against Mexicans and Latinos are the work of extremist white supremacist groups that often attract individuals with mental health disorders and manipulate them to carry out their horrible deeds. Such acts, as I stated previously, are not by any means the systemic racist atrocities of the vast majority of people in the U.S. or any of its institutions. Just for the record, I do not believe that there is widespread institutional racism, as some politicians have recently stated, at this time in the history of this young nation. The U.S. has from its founding significantly progressed in terms of human and civil rights, and currently offers residents, citizens, and millions of immigrants from every corner of the world a home and opportunities for prosperity, the pursuit of happiness, and their chance at attaining "The American Dream." We can both acknowledge and investigate the atrocities and rampant racism intrinsically tied to the U.S. in the past and also recognize and celebrate how far the "Melting Pot" has come. That doesn't mean we don't have any more progress to make. But it does mean that race should not be the first and foremost thing we think about, talk about, and use to examine every single thing in life.

Once again, if you disagree with me, I respect your opinion. No matter these more personal beliefs, while reading this narrative, I challenge the reader to consider the following questions:

- Do Mexicans today constitute a neglected minority in the U.S., especially in the current national social, economic, and political dialogue? If you answer in the affirmative, then why? The answer to this may constitute an entire separate essay!

- Are Mexicans and Latinos today contributing to or taking more than their fair share from the U.S.? This question should include residents, citizens, and undocumented individuals.

- Has the American Dream been achieved at the expense of Mexicans and Latinos?

- Has the American Dream been hindered by the historic treatment of Mexicans and other Latinos?

Perhaps to most people who are not of Mexican decent or from other Latin countries, the answers to these questions are not so apparent on the surface. Is it safe to say that beyond shallow stereotypes, most Anglos and African Americans know very little about who the Mexicans and other Latinos are from a historical and cultural standpoint? I do not mean this in an insulting way, but I'm just stating a fact that has been apparent to me over the last 30 plus years.

Or how about this last question: Is the American Dream being achieved today *because of* significant contributions by Mexicans and Latinos?

Each of you may already have a variety of opinions about the above questions. In this work titled *The Neglected Minority, Do Mexicans Matter?* I strive to provide the reader with a historical overview of the Mexican people that initially came to populate the various regions that we know today as the United States of America. You can decide for yourself how Mexicans have been treated during the four eras that will be described in this narrative. I invite you to consider if Mexicans have been and/or continue to be largely neglected in the current national American dialogue, and ultimately if Mexicans matter beyond providing essential manual labor.

To that effect, I shall provide an outline which hopefully takes the reader on a journey of learning about the history of Mexicans, Mexican Americans, and other Latinos who have chosen to make the U.S. their home. I will also outline the current status of this minority in our society. The discussion will take us along four main eras. The first era spans from the time of the Conquest of Mexico, resulting in some 300 years of Spanish Rule (1521-1821). The second is the shortest, encompassing Mexico's independence from Spain (1821-1848). The third era traces the events that followed the end of the Mexican American War in 1848, the so-called "Early American Period," to 1968, and includes the critical civil rights struggle. Finally, we'll explore the final era, from 1968 to the present, the so-called "Modern Era." Especially in the third and fourth eras, this work emphasizes the collision of the Anglo and Hispanic/Mexican cultures, which are vastly different and often resulted in catastrophic consequences still pertinent to this day.

I apologize in advance to other Latino groups that are as critically important as Mexicans to the present and future of the United States for focusing my narrative mostly on the history of Mexicans. I am of Mexican descent and this is the history my family has experienced. My grandfather cultivated in me a curiosity for knowledge that still burns deeply inside along with the deep-rooted belief in being proud of our ancestry and of who we are. I want to share with all people of Mexican decent, and other minorities too, that it is not enough to be satisfied with being an American citizen or resident in the U.S., but to lift your head high and feel an enormous sense of dignity and pride in who you are, where you came from, and what you bring to this country, culturally and economically, never accepting an underclass status or designation.

This work is not meant to be a strict scholarly article that replaces or discredits in any fashion academic research by historians of each period or events covered in the text. I do not pretend to be an historian or an academic on these topics, just a humble individual curious and interested in Mexican-American history and what it can teach us so we can avoid the mistakes of the past as well as highlight and acknowledge the progress that has been accomplished.

If you are a young second, third, or fourth generation Mexican American and you have not had the opportunity to read about your family's roots, may this book illustrate where you and your family came from and the important place this American society holds for you and your children. Please do not hesitate to look deeper and to critically research for yourself each era as you may wish to do so.

> We examine our history to see what it can teach us so we can avoid the mistakes of the past.

If you are of Anglo descent or another ethnicity and live in the U.S., I hope this work serves to help you gain some degree of appreciation for Mexican Americans and other Latinos presently living in the U.S. and to put into perspective the history of my people in the U.S. This history is all too often unknown, neglected, and frequently unappreciated, yet now more than ever important to a group of people occupying a role of unavoidable social and economic importance in all aspects of U.S. society. Perhaps this work will inspire the reader to know more about the Mexicans and Latinos in the U.S., not merely as the indisputable labor backbone of the country, but as a growing, diversely educated minority that will not allow itself to continue to be relegated to the trash bin of neglect or as an afterthought in the raging current U.S. climate of cultural, racial, and political debate.

So, are Mexicans neglected? Or do Mexicans matter? You tell me!

THE FOUR ERAS

In the following chapters, we'll briefly examine four time periods, or eras, in the history of Mexican Americans in the U.S. The first era comprises the time of Spanish rule from 1521-1821, the year Mexico gained its independence. The second era spans the brief time of Mexican independence through the end of the Mexican-American War (1821-1848), when Mexico lost 55% of its territory to the U.S. with the signing of the Guadalupe Hidalgo Peace Treaty. These time periods serve to illustrate the formation of the Mexican nation, from the indigenous peoples inhabiting the Valley of Mexico, the forceful brutal mixing with the Spanish overlords, the rejection of heirs, and the caste system imposed upon them and their heirs, which significantly contributed to a submissive psyche still prevalent today.

The third era spans the next 120 years from 1848 to 1968. Of utmost importance in understanding the catastrophic and often violent collision of two different cultures, one feeling superior to the other, was a belief in a Manifest Destiny ordained by God, with a diverging vision for the future of America.

The fourth and final era, from 1968 to the present, has been a time of growing numbers and Mexican Americans significantly contributing to the economic growth and prosperity of the U.S., yet at times clearly marginalized and excluded from enjoying the full fruit of its benefits. One may ask what has been the impact of "The Great Society" and "War on Poverty" of the 1960s on Mexicans in the U.S. Undoubtedly, as a result of the Anglo societal pressure to assimilate and accept their role, Mexican Americans have redefined for themselves their own meaning of the "American Dream" out of necessity. Is it enough to conclude that most Mexicans and some other Latinos should just be grateful for being better off economically in the U.S., even as "unwanted foreigners," than in their friendlier but economically disadvantaged native lands?

Over the four eras mentioned above, have Mexican Americans been consistently treated as equal citizens, afforded equal rights, opportunities, and privileges under the law, not just in principle but in practice, as Anglo Americans and other Europeans? Could the case be made that in certain circumstances Mexican Americans since 1848, in spite of the assurances of the aforementioned Guadalupe Hidalgo Peace agreement between both nations, were treated almost as horrifically as African Americans?

I need to emphasize that I do not ever by any means imply that Mexicans suffered to the same degree as Native American peoples or African Americans through the outrageous sin of slavery, just that the cruel history of racial prejudice and discrimination directed at Mexican Americans is not nearly as well known by Anglo Americans as the well documented history of African Americans in the U.S.

What has changed over these eras? What do we need to lament and what do we need to celebrate?

With all of these issues in mind, and considering the resiliency and fortitude of character of the minority populations that inhabit the U.S., let's embark on a brief historical analysis of these four critically important time periods, such that we may hope to have a more humble and deeper understanding of our past and present. Thus, endowed with that knowledge and wisdom, may we in the U.S., unselfishly and smartly as Americans, choose to select the best path forward, together and solidly united.

> What do we need to lament and
> what do we need to celebrate?

THE SPANISH ERA
1521 - 1821

THE FIRST MEXICANS

To fully grasp who Mexican Americans are, we must first delve into the history of the Conquest of Mexico by the Spaniards. When Hernán Cortés arrived at Cozumel just off the coast of Yucatan in early March of 1519, he encountered friendly natives who quickly communicated that the Mayan Chief Nachán Can, located on the mainland at Chactemal, had two Spaniards that he had obtained as slaves some years earlier.

Cortés immediately sent letters to them, inquiring as to their whereabouts and situation. He invited them to join his expedition. Apparently, these men had been shipwrecked in a caravel sailing from Panama to Santo Domingo in 1511. The crew had drifted on the ship's lifeboat for two weeks until currents pushed them to the shore of what today is Quintana Roo, Mexico, where the few survivors were captured and enslaved by local Mayans. Eventually the two men would be acquired as slaves by Nachán Can. One of these was the Franciscan priest Jeronimo de Aguilar who became the chief's trusted advisor. After more than five years of loyal service he was offered his freedom, which he promptly accepted and joined Cortés.

The second man was Gonzalo Guerrero. He had been accepted as a loyal subject after proving himself in multiple battles alongside his new Mayan compatriots and on one occasion saving a Mayan warrior from certain death by an alligator. In time he had earned a lofty position in the Mayan town, that of military captain of Chectemal, dignified by prestigious facial and body tattoos and eventually married the chief's daughter, Zazil Ha. They had three children, the first Mexicans or mestizos (mixed race children). He had become enamored with the Mayan way of life, including their harmonious relationship with all aspects of their natural environment. He told Aguilar that he loved his new life with his wonderful wife and three beautiful children, without a doubt preferring to stay and not join the Spaniards. Interestingly, his wife Zazil Ha addressed Aguilar in an angry tone, warning him not to bother her husband and to get lost. I understand that it's a stretch, but is this where Mexicans get their initial, almost instinctual devotion to wife and family? In a 2016 Pew Research Center survey of Hispanic men, family-related priorities were cited as extremely important in life. Numbers one and two among these were being a good father and providing for one's family. It would appear Gonzalo Guerrero was a great role model, devoted to family, and apparently a great warrior who served the Mayan chief well in that capacity. His family's statue can be found today in the town of Akumal at the beach's entrance in Half Moon Bay, in close proximity to where the green sea turtles come to lay their eggs.

Hugging the coastline up the Gulf of Mexico towards the future city of Veracruz, the eleven ships of Spaniards skirmished with a local chief and his tribe in Tabasco. When the cannon fired and the horses appeared with Spanish men mounted in full armor, the natives scattered. As settlement, the chief gave Cortés and his 508 men twenty females to cook and for intimate company. One of these females would become instrumental to the success of the Spanish conquest and to the history of Mexico.

Malintzin was a teenager when she was given to the Spaniards. Some years earlier her father, a prominent chief of a marginal Aztec provincial village, had died as a result of having been poisoned by her mother and uncle who had entered into an adulterous affair. Malintzin was next in line to the throne, yet being a minor meant her mother and uncle, who were now married, became the acting rulers. When they had a male offspring, a plot was hatched to sell the young Malintzin to slave traders who eventually sold her to a Mayan tribe. She was later sold again to yet another chief in Tabasco. Her mother had held a mock funeral in front of the town's people when one of her servant's daughters had died and pretended that it was Malintzin who was being buried. Malintzin had been educated as a princess in the traditional Aztec hierarchy, was fluent in Nahuatl, their language, and subsequently learned several Mayan dialects.

SPEAKING TO STRANGERS

These valuable language skills would soon come to Cortés' attention when Moctezuma's emissaries arrived to interview the Spaniards. The priest Aguilar could not communicate, as he did not speak Nahuatl. Malintzin, who had been given to one of the men, came forward and was able to communicate fluently with the Aztec representatives, translate into a Mayan dialect understood by Aguilar, then he to Spanish for Cortés and then in reverse. From that moment on, she became the interpreter or, as some called her, "The Tongue," and Cortés took her back from the soldier who had become her master. In his 2019 book *Speaking to Strangers*, Malcolm Gladwell describes how difficult those initial back and forth communications must have been. Without a doubt, there was plenty of room for miscommunication, misunderstanding, and misperceptions. Thus, those involved often arrived at entirely inaccurate or at least partly incorrect assumptions about the other, especially with regards to the mysterious, all-powerful monarch across the sea that Cortés represented and that great God in the heavens above, ruler of the universe, who entrusted Cortés with the mission of converting them to his faith. These stories bring to mind the early interactions some 200 or so years ago between the Spanish Mexicans living for multiple generations in what would become the southwestern states and the English-speaking new arrivals. Two cultures initially attempting to understand the other, even with the best amicable intentions, were eventually likely to result in one forcefully dominating over the other, in part attributed to language and cultural misunderstandings.

Malintzin soon learned Spanish and was taught the basic edicts of the Christian faith, of which she found some aspects incomprehensible and incongruent, yet she converted and was baptized as Marina. Cortés no longer needed Aguilar, and, speaking with Marina directly, gained knowledge of local history and customs of the Aztecs and surrounding tribes. By miraculous providence he seized on a key detail that would become instrumental in the success of the conquest of the Aztecs and Mexico. Malintzin provided the critical information about Moctezuma's psychological vulnerabilities and the Aztec's many enemies who could be recruited to join the Spaniards. She and Cortés, who was 35 at the time, had begun a passionate love affair. She was promptly given the seat next to Cortés in all casual and official affairs and respectfully became known as Dona Marina, a title of the utmost respect usually reserved for women of the highest noble birth.

Aztecs scriptures foretold that one day, in the not-too-distant future, Quetzalcóatl, their all-powerful God and creator, would return to hold the warring Aztecs accountable. This feathered God was a tall, blonde-haired, powerful, all-wise being who had left centuries before with the promise of someday returning. There had been several omens, such as an eclipse of the sun, a drought, a plague, and a volcanic eruption, all indicating that the fateful day would soon be upon them. Montezuma became morose, withdrawn, and isolated with his thoughts, hardly speaking to anyone, ultimately frozen with doubt and inaction. He knew the Aztecs, who had become a war-like people, dominating the Valley of Mexico with ruthless efficiency, had not lived up to the standards of their God. Punishment would be forthcoming.

The royal priests stepped up their sacrifices. On one such four-day period, almost 80,000 lost their lives. But nothing relieved Montezuma's insomnia and asphyxiating anxiety. When news arrived that several floating houses and tall beasts had been spotted on the beaches near modern day Veracruz, Moctezuma went into a panic. He dispatched multiple loads of golden gifts, silver jewelry, precious stones, and rare delicate feathers, which only served to pique the greed of the Spaniards. Cortés became so emboldened that he wrote a letter directly to the Spanish king detailing the events thus far. Cortés had become aware of rumors among a good number of the men who feared the warring Aztecs would promptly and easily overtake them. To prevent a mutiny, he had the audacity to scuttle the ships. Cortés had confessed in private to Malintzin that the Spaniards had a fatal disease of the blood that only gold could possibly cure and they needed large doses! If Malintzin had doubts, especially about greed being at the core of this so-called disease, she kept them to herself, a trait so often present in the native Mexican character, and still pertinent to this day.

In total, the conquest of Mexico campaign lasted a mere two years, fought mainly Indian versus Indian, with Cortés and the Spaniards orchestrating most of the bloody action. Marina had been correct in cajoling various tribes to follow Cortés and prescient in understanding Moctezuma's fragile psyche, permitting his meek surrender and imprisonment in his own grandiose palace by the Spaniards. By the time the next Aztec leaders, Cuitláhuac and Cuauhtémoc respectively, took command, it was too late. The Spaniards had taken control of the capital city of Tenochtitlan. Some historians believe Moctezuma was stoned to death by his own people while others that he was murdered by a Spanish sword when he was no longer useful in keeping his people at bay. No matter, the natives felt the betrayal by their own leader.

In an attempt to uncover the hiding place of all the Aztec gold, Cortés had Cuauhtémoc tortured by burning his feet, but the brave young emperor never revealed any such treasure. Marina had represented to Moctezuma and the priests that Cortés and his men were descendants of Quetzalcóatl and it was their rightful kingdom for the taking. For this and other actions throughout the entire conquest, including saving the Spaniards early along the campaign on at least two occasions from certain defeat, Malintzin has been labeled a traitor. Over the centuries she has been called "Malinche" by most Mexicans since phonetically this sounded like her native name. This acquired a derogatory meaning, in essence to be called a "Malinchista" is to be accused of being a traitor to one's own people.

In contrast, Cuauhtémoc and Cuitláhuac remain larger than life heroes in Mexico. Mexicans who immigrated to the U.S. at times have been labeled "Malinchistas" by the educated that remained in Mexico, fueling a rift with allegations that those north of the border have gradually become ignorant of Mexican customs, language, and history, thinking that Cinco de Mayo (celebrating victory over the French when they invaded Mexico) and 16th of September (celebrating the start of the Mexican War for Independence, and said in English because the Spanish – Diesiseis de Septiembre – is much more difficult for English speakers) celebrations are all there is to know about their rich native land.

GOLD FOR GOD

The aftermath of the conquest did not go well for the native populations. The Spaniards, as the new masters of these most fertile territories, and perhaps out of blind greed, failed to see or take interest in how these indigenous populations had existed for thousands of years in a symbiotic relationship with their natural habitat. To feed millions of people the natives had cultivated corn, or maize, for more than 7000 years, having bred the first corn from wild grasses. Were the Spaniards curious about tomatoes, avocados, jicama, nopales, chiles, limes, and many other vegetables and fruits native to Mexico that these so called "savages" consumed in their daily diets? Did they take the time to study the architectural, agricultural, and calendar advancements, in many cases superior to anything in Europe, that the Aztecs had innovated? Yes, the Aztecs even had the use of the wheel, but it was implemented in children's toys. It was of almost no use to them since they did not have beasts of burden.

Sadly, the initial conquerors were not highly enlightened men, more like rudimentary adventurers seeking a shallow golden fortune, almost oblivious to the true surrounding beauty of this strange land and its people. (And perhaps the Romans were the only empire of conquerors who ever respected and even adopted some customs from the people they subjugated.) Their priests offered the concept of a single almighty God and the promise of a glorious afterlife to the surviving Aztecs. I doubt any Spaniard considered the superior Aztec diet and hygiene, from a health perspective, or that perhaps corn would in time feed billions across the world. They had no clue that tomatoes, onions, and hot peppers, mixed with cilantro and plenty of fresh avocados, served on a tortilla with beef, pork, or chicken would one day conquer the world's palates. This would be the real business! These Spaniards, without a doubt blind to such cultural culinary riches, only had eyes for silver, gold, and other fine gems.

The reality is that more than 75% of the natives ultimately died from the smallpox epidemic and other European viral illnesses that swept the entire Valley of Mexico. The survivors, forced into submission, were immediately enslaved. Furthermore, the Spaniards destroyed all the indigenous religious icons, creating mass despair, with priests forcefully converting the surviving Indians to their version of the Catholic faith by any means possible. When this proved more difficult than anticipated, they used the image of the brown-skinned Virgin of Guadalupe as their patron saint, after she allegedly had appeared and spoken several times to the simple peasant Juan Diego. When he brought back proof for the priests to see, consisting of the sudden appearance of the image of the Virgin etched on his beige, long apron, previously filled with the never-before-seen red roses the Virgin had told him to pick, the peasants finally converted. Some say in her eyes one can see the reflection of the priests present that day. A miracle, as many Mexicans believe, or a marketing stroke of genius by Spanish priests, remains a debatable point in Mexican history.

In another unfortunate pattern of injustice, many of the Spaniards had taken indigenous women by force, resulting in unwanted pregnancies and the birth of more mestizo children, who were

34

rejected by both cultures. The psychological impact on the self-esteem of these children, who would become the majority of Mexicans, was critically analyzed in Octavio Paz's 1950 *The Labyrinth of Solitude*, a masterpiece concerned with the Mexican struggle with identity. Having inherited two cultures, the indigenous and the Spanish, yet in the end, by rejecting one or the other or both, the Mexican psyche becomes stuck in a world of endless solitude. Who am I and where do I belong?

The Mexican's main protection from feeling completely alone in the world comes from family and community with those that are like him. The fiestas, the constant celebrations, the family gatherings, the Day of the Dead, the religious gatherings, are all intended to, at least for a moment, deny the deep burden of solitude frequently experienced by those with the least education. For many such Mexicans, living outside of their culture and their comforting surroundings is especially traumatic. In addition to the above, the accusation of being "Malinchistas," no longer accepted by Mexicans south of the border, fuels deep feelings of rejection. These real psychological issues for Mexican Americans are of utmost importance in understanding the uneven relationship throughout history between Mexicans and Anglo Europeans, especially in the post 1848 era.

THE BETRAYAL

For Marina, her relationship with Cortés deteriorated rapidly after the birth of their son Martin. As it turned out, Hernán Cortés, now named Marques del Valle de Oaxaca, had been married to a

Spaniard since 1516. Her name was Catalina Suárez and she had been patiently waiting in Cuba. When Cortés finally told Marina that his wife was coming to New Spain, as Mexico would be renamed, in a fit of fury she swore he would never touch her again and left with the child. When he went to beg her to return to the palace where he had been living with her, she refused. When he professed his love for her, she refused to see him.

Cortés had also been betrayed by the Spanish crown. A high-ranking nobleman, Antonio de Mendoza, was made Viceroy. Cortés would not be in control of the new lands. Shortly after his wife arrived in 1522, during a celebratory dinner, she suffered a severe asthmatic attack that resulted in her death. Some believe Cortés himself applied his thumbs to her throat, depriving the poor lady of air. When Cortés went to tell Marina of the unfortunate events, she saw through his insincere intentions and once again turned him away. Marina eventually married a common soldier and had a child with him. It is believed that on one occasion when she traveled side by side with Cortés, leading a large army around the town of her birth, her mother recognized her and promptly threw herself at her feet begging for forgiveness. Cortés asked her if she wanted to punish her mother and uncle for their actions with death. Marina, in her typical magnanimity, looking at Cortés with piercing disdain, dismounted her horse, and embraced the weeping mother, comforted her, and finally forgave her with a gentle kiss.

At some point, Cortés decided that their son Martin should be educated by a caretaker and he was eventually taken to Spain. In 1529, Cortés managed to obtain from Pope Clement II a papal bull legitimizing Martin Cortés as his legitimate son and heir. In time, Cortés married a Spanish aristocrat who bore him in a son in 1532, whom he also named Martin, and it was he who inherited his father's titles and estates, not Marina's son. She passed away at about 29 years of age, apparently a victim of smallpox. If only Shakespeare would have known about Malintzin's exceptional life, then we may have had the good fortune of a most remarkable tragic play, perhaps rivaling Shakespeare's McBeth. Is she the mother of a most unique people, the one that facilitated the sprouting of Christianity in the Americas, or the traitor of millions of indigenous people? Or both? Mexicans to date continue to struggle with these questions.

With this history of the conquest as a background, let's now move towards the arrival of African people into Mexico, brought as slaves or personal servants, a chapter in the history of New Spain that until recently has received little attention.

AFRICAN SLAVES IN MEXICO

The history of the Afro-Mexicans, as they have come to be known, is an important chapter of the colonial period. Approximately 5% of Mexican's DNA comes from Africa and about 1.2% of the current Mexican population has African ancestry. There were some 200,000 African slaves brought by the Spaniards to New Spain, starting in 1519, with the largest numbers from 1580 to 1640. Those initially brought with the conquistadors were personal servants or concubines of their Spanish masters. Many of these Spaniards had been second or third born sons, who would not inherit family assets or titles back in Spain, had risked it all on an adventure to acquire vast wealth with a plan to return to Spain to purchase estates and titles of nobility. To have slaves attend to their every personal need had become a status symbol. In fact, six such Black individuals came with the Cortés expedition, one of which has allegedly been blamed for the transmission of smallpox to the natives. As an institution, in theory, slavery was forbidden by the crown except for cases of rebellion. However, it turned out that indigenous people were enslaved via coerced labor in the encomienda system that provided private land grants to Spanish born individuals living in New Spain. A forgotten fact was that Black overseers were frequently made to supervise the indigenous workers, all too often resulting in maltreatment of the Indians by overloading them with excessive tasks, taking them away from their lands and ultimately causing some natives to die at their hands. In some communities, Blacks were not permitted contact with the indigenous populations, especially to prevent harm to the women. Fines and lashes were typical penalties for such infractions. When Blacks rebelled against the Spanish masters, these were hanged, as occurred in 1537 in Mexico City. There wasn't a class separation of just the wealthy/powerful and the poor/oppressed, but a multi-level system of hierarchy that was often more complex than we have traditionally learned.

When the indigenous population started to dwindle toward the latter part of the century, on account of the viral epidemics, poor treatment, and worsening nutrition, African slaves were bought in to fill the gaps, especially in the silver mines, agricultural fields, and domestic labor. Slave ownership, especially in domestic duties, became a status symbol for elite Spanish women.

YANGA THE GREAT

In time many slaves purchased their freedom from the Spanish masters. Others became runaways, heading south towards modern day Guerrero and Oaxaca. A few contested their status by rebellion. The most famous was a group led by Gaspar Yanga, who battled the Spanish near Veracruz for nearly 40 years, finally recognized as independent in 1608, making it the first community of free Blacks in America. Yanga's statue stands to this day. Since the vast numbers of slaves were men, over the following centuries they mixed with indigenous and Spanish populations. By the 17th century, the free Black population outnumbered enslaved individuals and the growing presence of mixed-race people was socially evident. Slave trade into Mexico officially came to an end in 1640. By then, Mexico City had become home to the most diverse community that included poor Spaniards, indigenous Mexicans, mestizos, and Blacks, all serving wealthy Spaniards in a variety of capacities. Since the late 1500s, the Catholic Church had imposed forced indoctrination and assimilation, the shared stated goals of colonial authorities, inevitably distancing indigenous and Black populations from their traditions and pasts. In time the church became the center of these communities, strictly observing and following the priest's traditional Spanish Catholic dogma. The church was instrumental in imprinting the daily work ethic on the indigenous people, mostly to the benefit of the Spanish elite, with a clear message to endure earthly hardship now with heavenly rewards in the afterlife. Over 300 years of Spanish rule in Mexico, the mostly illiterate indigenous and rapidly growing mestizo populations submissively adapted and acquiesced to the harsh encomienda system, performing the brutal daily manual labor on behalf of the Spanish overlords, while mostly accepting the Catholic Church's and well-meaning pastor's aforementioned social contract.

THE SPANISH CASTE SYSTEM

Starting in the 1500s, the Spanish — under Hapsburg rule for some 200 years, then the Bourbons for another 50 years — established in New Spain a racist social caste system, a "pigmentocracy," with the whiter Spaniards born in Spain at the top of the hierarchy, then those born in Mexico from Spanish parents, the Criollos, and then lower the Mestizos, and trapped at the bottom the indigenous peoples, especially those with African ancestry. Aristotle's ideology that some people were born slaves, benefiting by a life of servitude under civilized masters was the adopted European status quo. Bartolomé de las Casas, known as "The Apostle of the Indians," attended the 1550 Valladolid congress organized by the Spanish crown to discuss the nature and status of the indigenous American populations. Theologians, jurists, and government officials determined that these noble savages, docile and open to conversion to Catholicism, were in fact human, yet of limited intelligence and capacity for higher learning.

In theory, slavery of these peoples was made illegal, but not their subjugation and exploitation. De las Casas' arguments that the inhumane abuses were not in accordance with God's edicts, based after having spent years in Mexico fighting with Spanish authorities on behalf of the natives, had not been completely accepted.

Furthermore, racist governmental and social institutions established by the Spanish, aimed mainly at financing Spain's many European conflicts, were by the late 1700s mostly antiquated from a political, social, economic, and intellectual standpoint. After a brief economic boom in the mid- to late- 1700s from a reorganization of the silver mines, Spain was almost bankrupt. As last resort, imperial free trade was attempted from 1778 to 1789, but the maneuver failed. Spain would be ill prepared to control and hold onto the colonies. By this time a larger Criollo and mestizo population had emerged, far outnumbering the roughly 10% Spanish born, and wanted to assert control of their own destiny. These educated individuals were aware of the continuing exploitation of the indigenous and Black populations that had largely mixed. The older Spanish caste system was gradually disappearing, in part replaced by one based on socioeconomic factors as more important than race in determining individual social rank. To date, this system still persists in modern Mexico, with many immigrants to the U.S., especially from the southern Mexican states, still affected by such forms of discrimination and racism. By the time the war of Mexican Independence started in September of 1810, the leading mestizos of the day had become aware of the French Revolution's outcome and the American colonies' successful establishment of their own independent United States. When Napoleon Bonaparte invaded Spain, an opportunity presented itself. Before discussing the Mexican period from 1821 to 1848, let us first examine the migration of people from New Spain to what would become the southern states in the U.S.

POPULATING THE NORTHERN MEXICO TERRITORIES

In 1540, Francisco Vásquez de Coronado marched into the Rio Grande valley with 230 Spanish soldiers, some 800 indigenous Mexican men, and 3 women. The first expedition into California was in 1542, arriving in modern day Santa Barbara. The search for the fabled Seven Cities of Gold led to many explorers arriving in Arizona in 1539. However, full colonization did not occur till 1598 when the Catholic Church in Spain demanded the conversion of indigenous people to the Catholic faith. The initial settlement was led by Juan Oñate, who established a permanent settlement in Española, New Mexico, just north of Santa Fe. Not long after Oñate's settlement, my own family arrived in northern New Mexico. Generous land grants had been approved from the Viceroy of New Spain to relocating Spanish families. Most had come from Spain in search of a new life. With rumors of precious metals, especially gold, it had not been difficult to recruit new settlers into the new world. When none of the gold or silver was ever found, the settlers built tight knit agricultural communities in northern New Mexico. When a conflict ensued in 1680 with the Pueblo people uprising against the Spanish settlers, these moved back south and founded modern day El Paso.

Around 1692, Diego de Vargas brought the settlers on the re-conquest of northern New Mexico, with half my family staying in El Paso and the other half moving back up north. These family members of mine on my father's side were one of several families given a land grant and deeds to a tract that would become known as the Las Vegas land tract. It consisted of approximately 496,446 acres of land in New Mexico that included the modern-day Santa Fe, Albuquerque, and the town of Las Vegas (not that Las Vegas!). The families who had settled in those regions prior to the Pueblo revolt and had returned after the conflict had been resolved, began to establish themselves once again as farmers and ranchers. This went on through the early 1800s. I will return to this matter in the next section of this work.

The first Spanish settlements in Arizona were in 1691 and in California in 1769. The Presidio of San Diego, founded by Father Junípero Serra, signaled the beginning of the brutally oppressive mission system, mostly against the indigenous populations. The first missions in Texas were founded in the 1680s and moved into east Texas in the 1690s. For the most part, settlements were sparsely populated with families functioning largely independent and out of reach of Spanish authorities in Guadalajara and Mexico City. These isolated communities depended on agriculture and ranching with occasional intermingling and trading with various local indigenous populations. Waves of Spanish born immigrants and the growing mestizo population were readily accepted into these settlements, while totally indigenous peoples were discriminated against. Native American populations were frequently dispossessed of lands and territories that had been part of their heritage for perhaps thousands of years. They too were systematically branded as subhuman savages that must be subjugated and indoctrinated into the Catholic faith, willingly or by force if necessary. It was not surprising that some tribes would frequently rebel against the new arrivals. The Spanish social caste system had been retained with the Native Americans relegated to the bottom. The Catholic Church, at the center of each of these northern communities, with elite families from direct Spanish descent and a few educated mestizos at the top, controlling church and key local government positions, acquiesced to this caste system mostly to the detriment of the Mexican indigenous populations and Native Americans.

TIME FOR INDEPENDENCE

In 1810, the Mexican War for Independence began with the still celebrated 16th of September "Cry for Independence" by the Jesuit priest Miguel Hidalgo y Costilla. The war culminated with the signing of the Treaty of Cordoba on August 24, 1821. The leaders of the conflict who had promoted the killing of Spaniards, or "Gachupines" as they were derogatively called, had been mostly mestizos at the front of disorganized and untrained hordes of illiterate, indigenous Mexicans. These mestizo leaders were tired of a secondary citizen status and in some instances, such as in Hidalgo's and Morelos' cases, actually cared about the plight of the indigenous people. The leaders were in time captured by Spanish loyal forces, given quick trials and put to death by a firing squad, eventually becoming martyrs with official historians firmly engraving them in the pantheon of Mexican national heroes. Priests Hidalgo, a Criollo, and his protégé Morelos, both sacrificed their lives in the struggle for basic human rights and the welfare of the Mexican native populations.

Paradoxically, the 40-year-old Agustín de Iturbide, an army general fighting on behalf of the Spaniards, in 1821 switched sides to join the rebel army led by General Vicente Guerrero. This was in reaction to a liberal coup d'état in Spain that resulted in Mexican conservatives, who had till that point been staunch royalists, to immediately demand independence. In short time, the three guarantees that formed Iturbide's Plan de Iguala secured the secession from Spain on August 24,1821. Iturbide quickly removed General Guerrero and his followers from positions of influence, became president of the Regency, and a year later crowned himself "Constitutional Emperor of Mexico," Agustin I. He reigned arbitrarily and extravagantly and was unable to bring order and stability to the nascent country. General Antonio López de Santa Anna galvanized the opposition that called for the overthrow and exile of Iturbide, who soon abdicated and was exiled in 1823 to Italy, then to England. Returning to Mexico in 1824 to offer his services in case of a Spanish invasion, Iturbide was unaware that congress had previously decreed his death. On arrival, he was promptly arrested and executed. This was but the start of more than twenty years of political upheavals, mainly due to oscillations of power between Liberals and Conservatives, wanting a federalist republic as opposed to an independent monarchy, resulting in at least twenty-one different presidents in that time period. So much chaos reigned in Mexico that incredibly the infamous Antonio Lópes de Santa Anna, perhaps among the worst presidents or leaders any country has ever had, would sit on the presidential chair eleven times, much to the detriment of Mexico and those at the Alamo!

THE MEXICAN ERA 1821-1848

After 1821, the northern Mexican states of California, Arizona, New Mexico, Utah, Colorado, and Texas remained sparsely populated. Given the distance from the center of control in Mexico City, authorities encouraged citizens to engage in economic trade with Americans. This freedom brought inevitable social and economic ties between elites in these states and citizens of the United States. Interestingly, the Adams-Onis Treaty, also called the Florida Treaty, signed in 1819 between Spain and the U.S., ceded Florida to the U.S. and defined the boundary between the two countries. Spain was acting in self-interest and not Mexico's to finance conflicts in Europe. After Mexico had gained its independence, the Treaty of Limits between Mexico and the U.S. was signed in 1828 and made effective in 1832, recognizing the original Adams-Onis boundary. In other words, the understanding was: hands off previously owned Spanish lands. These matters would become of critical importance in the following decades.

The Mexican constitution of 1824 was based on the Constitution of Cadiz for American issues and on the U.S. Constitution for the formula for federal representation and organization. It guaranteed the equality of all Mexicans, regardless of race. Two key issues made it different form the U.S. Constitution. First, it declared the abolishment of slavery in Mexico. Second, it proclaimed the Roman Catholic Church as the official religion, making Catholicism protected by law and prohibiting any other.

President Vicente Guerrero, himself a "dark" Mexican, probably due to his African ancestry, made the decree of abolition of slavery effective in 1829. This issue caused serious consequences in California when Native Americans in Santa Barbara rebelled against the brutally abusive mission system, resulting in the secularization of mission lands and the eventual distribution through land grants to the wealthiest families in the state (1833), mostly those of elite Spanish descent. These new landowners needed a labor force to work their vast estates. Mexican citizens, mostly indigenous people that had migrated from the southern part of Mexico, soon became peasant laborers in the newly created haciendas. These estates mimicked the Southern U.S. plantations, and the workers often received worse treatment than the black slaves. With permission from the central government, Anglo immigrants and businessmen flooded the various states, mainly Texas and California, with marriages between Anglo men and Mexican women solidifying loyalties. These Americans had been welcomed with the condition of respecting Mexican constitutional laws. By 1835, Americans that had settled in the northern Mexican territories in increasing numbers revolted in Texas and declared independence from Mexico as "The Republic of Texas." Many of these were slave owners, such as Steven F Austin, in direct violation of Mexican law. This galvanized Santa Anna to march with the Mexican army to put down the revolt. After initial victories at The Alamo and Goliad, Santa Anna surrendered on April 26, 1836. Mexico refused to recognize the treaties signed by Santa Anna since he was a hostage under duress at the time. Consequently, the Republic of Texas was not recognized by Mexico as a sovereign state. Mexican citizens in Texas, mostly illiterate indigenous people, known as Tejanos, soon experienced discrimination on social, educational, and economic fronts. This was the situation in 1845 when James Polk became president of the United States.

WE SAY WE ARE SUPERIOR

The Monroe Doctrine, written by future president John Quincy Adams and presented to Congress by President James Monroe in 1823, showed the world the U.S. mindset. It was both a policy of protectionism and expansionism. The ideology contained within the document grew from the birth of a new exceptional nation built upon an untried political system, breaking from the past and embracing a unique new future. America for Americans! No longer could a European power interfere with or colonize in America without such action being considered an act of war against the U.S. Additionally, the Monroe Doctrine was based on a racial hierarchy with the white race considered superior, chosen by God, and at the top of the pyramid, with all others below in a subservient role. This Manifest Destiny would entitle the inevitable expansion westward to one day encompass all lands from ocean to ocean. After all, the English, who had warred against Spain for centuries, at times raiding gold and silver ships, had handed down to the Americans their hatred for Spain.

Like the Spanish, they saw the indigenous peoples as subhuman, like savage beasts of burden. From early on some of the founders, Jefferson and Adams among them, were not only bigots and slave owners, but had designs on seizing from Spain the rest of the American continent. Florida was the first, obtained from Spain in 1819, just prior to Spain finally relinquishing Mexico in 1821. Further emboldened, President Andrew Jackson signed the Indian Removal Act in 1830. The Native Americans residing east of the Mississippi were forcefully moved to modern day Oklahoma. This Trail of Tears, an act of extreme inhumanity, demonstrated the attitude of no longer needing to negotiate agreements or consider the desires of the Native Americans. The white superior race would decide for them.

LET'S JUST TAKE IT

When Texas was annexed in 1845, Mexico terminated diplomatic relations with the U.S. President Polk tried to negotiate twice, to settle residual border disputes and offer to purchase Alta, California, and the Santa Fe territories. Mexican authorities refused to meet with his emissaries. Undeterred, Manifest Destiny and political uncertainty in Mexico as the guiding principles, President Polk instructed General Zachary Taylor to provoke a war. A skirmish, later dubbed the Thornton Affair, at an abandoned hacienda occurred in April 1846. The killing of fourteen men, six wounded and one fatally wounded Americans and capture of eighty others on "American" territory by the Mexican army served as the primary justification Polk used to convince Congress to go to war. When Congressman Abraham Lincoln asked for the exact spot where American blood had been spilled, no one could actually say with certainty. Where those territories that rightfully belonged to Mexico? This question was never answered. (Today, Brownsville, TX, where the clash occurred, sits on the border of Texas and Mexico.)

The vote was thirty-six Democrats in favor of war and fourteen Whigs against. One senator stated that the war was an act of aggression against Mexico, literally at gunpoint. Future Presidents Ulysses S. Grant and Dwight D. Eisenhower readily admitted the grotesque, intentional abuse against a weakened country; certainly not a proud moment for the United States of America.

THE EARLY AMERICAN ERA 1848-1968

ONE-WAY TREATY

The Mexican-American War took place from 1846 to 1847, and concluded with the signing of the Treaty of Guadalupe Hidalgo on February 2, 1848. Mexico lost 55% of its territory, immediately ceded to the U.S. This treaty has had dramatic effects on the history of Mexican Americans to this day. The treaty promised equal citizenship rights under the American Constitution for the 80,000 plus Mexicans living in the ceded territories. These areas included Alta, California, Arizona, New Mexico, and parts of Utah, Nevada, and Colorado, significantly increasing the size of the U.S. It was agreed that Mexico would also relinquish any claim on Texas and that the new border between the two countries would be the Rio Grande. These Mexican peoples, whose families in many instances had lived on such territories for centuries, were welcome to stay as U.S. citizens with up to one year to declare such status. In addition, Article X of the treaty guaranteed the rights of holders of land grants to maintain ownership of such properties. Unfortunately, some of what would become the key details, adversely affecting these new "Americans," were in the treaty's fine print. As written, no legal guarantees were actually negotiated that would treat these Mexicans as full citizens under U.S. law. The U.S. Naturalization Act of 1790 said that only whites could become citizens, preventing most of the Mexican citizens in the newly acquired U.S. land from being welcomed in their new country.

Rampant and widespread discrimination, as well as violence, soon became commonplace, resulting in about 25% of these "Treaty Citizens" returning to Mexico. In anticipation of these abuses, Mexican President de Herrera had passed the recolonization plan of 1848, offering land and money to returning Mexicans. In New Mexico, formal legal barriers were soon bought forth to prevent this repatriation since the Mexican Americans served as a "civilized" buffer between the Anglo settlers and the Native American "encroachers." In addition, there was a treaty article about land ownership. As long as land grants and deeds could be produced and proven, all too often an extremely difficult task, people could hold on to their property. This article gave many false hopes. If the landowners possessed titles or grants in Spanish, or the land in question was not perfectly demarcated by an approved survey, they were deemed invalid. Such disputes were often dragged through the various court systems for years at an exorbitant cost, which far more often determined the outcome, rather than the legality and merits of each case. In time these Mexican Americans across all the ceded territories were dispossessed of vast amounts of ancestral lands. A few Spanish elites and affluent mestizos were the only ones capable of financing such lengthy quarrels. The non-assimilated, illiterate Mexicans, mostly made up of indigenous populations, were easily removed from their lands and subjected to the prevalent American racist system of the times, and were frequently exploited almost as badly as the Blacks.

MY LAND BY ANY MEANS

The aftermath of the Treaty of Guadalupe Hidalgo ushered in more than a century of second-class citizenship status and abuses aimed at these new citizens, the Mexican Americans. By 1850 the most common occupations of the treaty citizens were farmer, laborer, and servant. A three-tier society immediately emerged in Texas with the smallest number comprised of landed Anglos and a few Spanish elites as owners of large haciendas. Small landowners tending to individual ranchos made up the middle tier and the bottom rung of a vast number of peons living in "jacales," rudimentary huts made of mud and straw, whose social status was below free citizens and just barely above slaves. Anglos migrating into the area from the northeast saw this last group as primitive and subhuman. In California during the early American period, genocide killed almost 90% of the indigenous people, including Native Americans, clearing a path for

Anglo colonization.

GOLD RUSH FOR ANGLOS ONLY

Disenfranchisement and land loss was frequently achieved by seizing political and judicial power throughout the U.S. Southwest. The California Foreign Miner Tax, instituted during the Gold Rush, charged Mexicans and Chinese $20 a month mining fee, but exempted Europeans, diminishing competition from these unwelcomed "foreigners." The Land Act of 1851 resulted in the dispossession of lands since it became nearly impossible to prove the validity of the initial land grant and that improvements had been made. Anglo squatters were free to claim land for themselves, especially if they had made "improvements." Cases were extremely expensive and lengthy, with a seventeen-year average time for resolution, full of legal discrimination and predictably resulting in the loss of the land. My own family had been involved in such a legal case for what became known as the Las Vegas Land Grant. A relative of mine and several other families put forth a suit in 1835 to prevent Anglo squatters from obtaining ownership of nearly 500,000 acres of land near Santa Fe, New Mexico, appraised at two million dollars. In spite of the fact that the grant had existed since the late 1600s and was confirmed by the surveyor general of New Mexico in 1860, the case got "trapped" in the courts until the Supreme Court of the U.S. in 1901 ruled in favor of the Town of Las Vegas, without any compensation to the original grantees or their families. This was the pattern of the early American period.

Violence was a frequently used strategy to control the conquered Mexican Americans. After all, could the U.S. trust these new treaty citizens? Would they be more loyal to Mexico to the detriment of the U.S? Would they one day rise up against the U.S? These were concerns raised by many politicians and community leaders. Mexicans were simply not to be trusted. They must be marginalized at any cost and by any tactic. In California, between 1849 and 1860, at least 163 Mexicans were lynched. Most of these incidents served to intimidate Mexicans and keep them from mining and competing against Anglos during the Gold Rush.

By 1852 the population in California had grown to 260,000 from a mere 8,000 in 1848, mostly consisting of new Anglo arrivals, facilitating the displacement and abuse of Mexicans already there. The vast majority were attacked and often killed without a trial, all too often for minor allegations, self-defense, or for defending others in an altercation. The first known California woman to be lynched was Josefa Segovia, who in 1851 shot and killed a white intruder attempting to assault her. She was hung from a tree a mere two hours after a mock trial and the indistinct name "Juanita" placed nearby in sad disregard to her identity. This was also the case of the folk hero, Juan Cortina, who in 1859 shot the Brownsville Marshall for brutalizing his ranch employees. His men occupied the town and after a standoff, The Texas Rangers and U.S. Army defeated him. However, he later escaped and crossed the border to eventually lead many raids in the 1860s to avenge Anglo wrongdoers. When folk songs known as "corridos" were composed about his adventures, the Mexican "Bandido" had been officially born.

THE NEGLECT OF MEXICANS AMERICAN LYNCHING

The almost unknown history of mob violence against Mexicans has recently come to light. In January 2000, the Roth Horowitz Gallery in New York City displayed a photographic exhibit titled "Lynching Photography in America." Widely acclaimed, it was later shown at the New York Historical Society and at the Martin Luther King, Jr. National Historic Site. The exhibit contained fifty-seven images and several artifacts related to lynching. These included photographs of forty-five African American victims, Anglo fatalities, and others relating mob murder against Sicilian, Jewish, and Chinese individuals. James Allen included these photographs in his book *Without Sanctuary*, a recent work on lynching in the U.S. This tragic pictorial, along with Phillip Dray's work *At the Hand of Persons Unknown: The Lynching of Black America*, highlighted the atrocities of mob violence. This latter book was a major best seller and won a prestigious literary award. In more than 500 pages, even though the author discusses mob violence against other ethnic groups, the word Mexican or Mexicans does not appear once. Furthermore, neither the photographic exhibit nor this detailed book on lynching expose or even discuss the extent to which the lynching of Mexicans occurred. In fact, this significant omission and apparent erasure from the historical record leaves the impression that Mexicans were not victimized by racially motivated mob violence. Nothing could be further from the truth. It is difficult to estimate the number of Mexicans lynched during the early American period.

The Tuskegee Institute, which contains the most comprehensive records on this topic, classified Mexican, Chinese, and Native American as "White," inhibiting accurate records and awareness of the race-based violence against Mexican Americans. From 1882 to 1951, the record shows 4730 victims killed by lynching. 1293 of them white and 3437 Black. The actual number of Mexicans is unknown. In the recent 2003 work titled "The Lynching of Persons of Mexican Origin or Descent in the United States" by William D. Carrigan and Clive Webb, the authors estimate that from 1880 to 1930 Mexicans were lynched at a rate of 27.4 per 100,000 and African Americans at a rate of 37.1 per 100,000. It is also known that from 1848 to 1879 Mexicans were lynched at a rate of 473 per 100,000, clearly having faced unparalleled danger from mob violence. During this period, extreme acts of cruelty and torture were also committed against Mexican victims of lynching, which included being shot, mutilated, and burnt. The identity of these individuals was often unimportant compared to the symbolic nature of the message as Anglos forcefully imposed their sovereignty. The fact was that whites felt that they were the higher race and the higher class. More frequent than not, the allegation of a crime committed by a Mexican was unsubstantiated, and the individual was lynched prior to a trial and mostly killed for just being Mexican.

GOOD OLD BOY TEXAS RANGERS

The Texas Rangers, founded in 1823 mostly to protect whites against Mexicans and Native Americans, killed hundreds to thousands of Mexicans, mostly in south Texas. Major incidents included the Porvenir Massacre on January 28, 1918, when the Texas Rangers and some ranchers shot fifteen innocent Mexicans, including two teens, apparently in retaliation for a suspected Pancho Villa raid at the Brite Ranch a month before. Only five Rangers lost their jobs. Two months later, two more Mexicans, a rancher, and a female servant, were killed by raiders at the nearby Neville Ranch. No arrests were made. Many similar incidents occurred during the years of the Mexican Revolution, mostly driven by a mistrust of border Mexicans and overt racist Anglo-European ideology. It was definitely "open season" on Mexicans, including those who were U.S. citizens.

The Bisbee deportation in 1917 was carried out by Arizona Rangers and government troops of some 1200 Mexican miners and their families protesting over harsh work conditions and low wages compared to whites. These Mexican Americans were taken to the desert by the company train, abandoned without food or water, and warned if they returned, they'd face certain death. Nationally, these individuals were labeled "traitors" since the U.S. was fighting WWI. These types of sentiments all too often came from the White House. When referring to the Americas, President William Howard Taft, in office from 1909-1913, stated, "The whole hemisphere will be ours in fact as, by virtue of our superiority of race, already is ours morally." This reflected the sentiments of Anglo elites in the U.S., some still smarting over the fact President Polk had not "gotten" the whole of Mexico in 1848.

In the post 1848 period, racism prevailed against minorities on account of their race, faith, the predominant Manifest Destiny mindset mostly among northeastern whites, and socioeconomic control and dominance of most sectors of the economy. The Mexican 300 plus year adherence to the Catholic Church was irrationally discriminated against by the mostly protestant Anglos, originating in the centuries-old conflicts between Spain and England. The Mexican Catholic Spanish-speaking clergy, often involved in the daily affairs of the congregation and community, were frequently replaced by Anglo clergy, who were less nurturing and more distant. The poorest of the community most often felt a spiritual vacuum as a result. Once most of these people had become peons and day laborers at the behest of the new landowners and bosses, collective self-esteem and worthiness plummeted even further. The few remaining wealthy and more accepted whiter "Spanish Mexicans" were able to integrate into the Anglo society, while remaining discriminatory of the masses of illiterate indigenous Mexicans. To a large degree, this socioeconomic form of racism, rooted in the earliest history of Spanish entrance into Mexican history, has remained a visible pattern in modern Mexico. In the early American period, the stereotypical image of a dirty, lazy, dumb, dishonest, and untrustworthy Mexican rapidly spread, propagated by the few remaining wealthy "white" landowner Mexicans.

As more economic control was obtained by Anglos throughout all the U.S. Southwestern territories through force or one-sided legal processes, Mexicans were displaced and had to accept, assimilate, and accommodate the perceived superior race. In many instances, Mexicans preferred to avoid Anglos altogether by living in separate communities, friendly to all the traditions of Mexican culture. Mexicans did, however, count their blessings for the fact that they were still better off than the slaves of the southern plantations. On occasion, groups, such as the White Caps in New Mexico in the 1870s, formed to protect Mexicans against the illegal confiscation of their lands. Another such uprising was the Salt War in El Paso during the 1870s when Anglos took over what had been public lands containing the salt pits. When they started charging Mexicans for the salt obtained from the pits a protest ensued that resulted in the Texas Rangers killing several Mexicans. When an Italian Catholic priest trusted by the Mexicans attempted to mediate, more Mexicans were killed and the priest ended up siding with the Anglos. The salt that had been free for centuries would no longer be free. This was another example highlighting the fact that since 1848, Anglo Americans had seized complete political and economic control in the U.S. Southwest. The Mexicans that elected to stay and become loyal U.S. citizens in less than 20 years were politically disenfranchised and subjected to large-scale land loss. Educational opportunities that would ensure upward mobility had been all but closed.

SEGREGATION FOR MEXICANS TOO

In the 1870s, schooling became a segregated institution. When a school official supporting segregation stated, "Mexicans are inferior in personal hygiene, ability, and economic outlook," Anglo parents agreed and did not allow their children to mix with these inferior beings. These "Mexican" schools were rare, poorly funded, and usually did not offer any education past elementary school. Most Mexican children ended up following their parents' occupation in the fields, farms, factories, construction, or in domestic roles. Few obtained higher education, as it had no apparent value since professional opportunities were simply not open to Mexicans. It was the standard Anglo perception that Mexican Americans were a foreign underclass, dumb second-class citizens wanted for their sweat, military service, and taxes, while rejecting their culture and offspring. Even through the 1940s, almost 80% of Mexicans in the U.S. attended underfunded, segregated schools. Finally, the Supreme Court case of Mendez vs Westminster School District legally desegregated schools in California in 1946. This rapidly spread throughout the rest of the country and set the stage for Brown vs Board of Education in 1954.

These significant steps forward in leveling the scholastic opportunity playing field were still countered by the persistent bullying, racism, and discrimination targeting most minorities. This, among multiple other social and economic issues, was brought into the national spotlight by African American leaders in the ongoing struggle for civil rights in the 1960s. Sadly, the first national bloody struggle for civil equality in the U.S. that had taken place some one hundred years before during the Civil War (1861 to 1865) had fallen far short of accomplishing the true equality promised to all citizens in the U.S. Constitution. Mexicans felt resentment toward the U.S. for the way they had been treated post 1848. Wealthy Mexican American landowners throughout the Southwest mostly supported the Confederacy, which benefited from the economic advantage of free black labor since they too had exploited and, in some cases, had imposed forced labor on Native Americans. For the most part, working class Mexicans and poor peasants, fearing a society and system of government that would continue to exploit people as slaves, fought on the side of the Union Army.

In total, some 20,000 Mexican Americans fought in the Civil

War, at times heroically contributing to the eventual Union victory. In March of 1862, the New Mexico Volunteers, a massive army made up of almost all Mexican American recruits, destroyed the Confederate supply train at the "Battle of Glorieta Pass," also called the "Gettysburg of the West," effectively ending the Confederate intent of taking over the American west. In south Texas, the already famous Juan Cortina was recruited to cross the border and make raids against Confederate troops and on one occasion even killed a Confederate judge. In fact, the final battle of the Civil War was fought near Brownsville, Texas, almost one month after the Confederate surrender by General Robert E. Lee at Appomattox in April 1865, with the Confederate army defeating the Union soldiers.

The reconstruction era of the 1870s brought more discrimination against Mexican Americans, mostly from the migration of massive numbers of white land speculators intent on the acquisition of large tracts of land. New legislation in New Mexico stipulated that landowners present evidence of original land grants in both Spanish and English. This proved difficult for most Mexicans who had become U.S. citizens in 1848 and whose families had been in those lands for hundreds of years. Most of these did not have the financial wherewithal to take on the intricate, lengthy, and all too often unfair American legal system usually tilted in favor of whites. This occurred to my family, eventually resulting in the loss of a huge land tract. The Las Vegas Land Tract had been appraised at two million dollars in 1835, so one must wander what those five hundred thousand acres would be worth today?

In Texas these conflicts resulted in race wars. All too often

Anglo vigilance committees would raid Mexican Tejano ranches, kill all the males, burn down all their buildings, and force remaining family members across the border. In 1877, the owner of King Ranch, Richard King, with the help of the Texas Rangers, employed brutality and coercive violence to steal surrounding lands belonging to Tejanos, and eventually grew his property to almost one million acres. These famous Texas Rangers were in fact acting as King's private security force by systematically intimidating Mexican Americans into selling their land or risk losing their life. In recent years there has been more awareness over the racist brutality of these infamous early versions of the Texas Rangers, especially with the 100th anniversary of the Porvenir affair. In the book *Gunpowder Justice: A Reassessment of the Texas Rangers*, authors Julian Samora, Joe Bernal, and Albert Peña highlight that from 1915 to 1920 the Texas Rangers killed up to 5000 innocent Mexicans for the singular crime of being Mexican. One must wonder what opinion Chuck Norris would have today of his 1993 show "Walker, Texas Ranger," when his martial arts skills "fighting for justice" against the "bad guys" gave him a clear advantage. I am not pointing a finger at Mr. Norris, but in similar fashion to the above writers and the families of the Porvenir massacre, I too am shining a spotlight on the much-neglected topic of undeniable systemic racism, violence, and exploitation of Mexican Americans during this dark era of U.S. history.

COMPROMISE, CORRUPT BARGAIN, AND BETRAYAL OF 1877

The 1876 U.S. presidential election would dramatically change for the worse the course of civil rights for African Americans. In a backroom deal, informally arranged by various Congressmen, the presidential chair was given to Republican Rutherford B. Hayes over Samuel J. Tilden. There had been allegations of election fraud and violence in Florida, South Carolina, and Louisiana, which initially resulted in a Tilden victory with 203-165 electoral votes. However, twenty electoral college votes were disputed from Oregon, resulting in a commission being appointed to resolve the matter. In the end, the twenty-vote swing gave the presidency to Hayes, who, as part of the Corrupt Bargain, would immediately withdraw federal troops from southern states. These had remained in the south since the end of the Civil War in 1865 to protect newly freed African Americans.

Hayes also agreed to include at least one southern Democrat in his cabinet. The south would also gain from northern investments to build the transcontinental railroad. However, from then on, the southern states remained free to impose the Jim Crow laws, immediately worsening discrimination against Black people, and essentially causing societal disenfranchisement and pushing back efforts for equality into the 1950s and 1960s. Mexican Americans in southern states would suffer these societal inequities in parallel with African Americans in the aftermath of what Blacks would call "The Betrayal" of 1877. Soon the atrocities of the infamous organization known as the Ku Klux Klan (KKK) emerged, as well as exclusion from political office for non-whites. The north had won the Civil War, but the south won Reconstruction, to the detriment of minorities. One can only imagine the different trajectory of race relations in the U.S.

if Tilden had been sworn in as president.

JOSE CROW, JIM'S COUSIN

The 1880s fostered an age of prosperity for the U.S., brought forth by the extensive network of railroads, most of which were built by Mexican and

> The north had won the Civil War, but the south won Reconstruction, to the detriment of minorities.

Chinese laborers. Prosperity in the southwest was chiefly attained by the ongoing Anglo migrants from the northeast. Mexican Americans continued to be discriminated against during these years, and were largely excluded from the tremendous economic boom experienced by Anglo-Americans. Segregation was in full force, marginalizing Mexicans in most aspects of the community, including the aforementioned schools. This came to be known as "Jose Crow." No, not an innovative form of smooth, original Tequila, but a parallel American social contract to the Jim Crow laws of the southern United States.

Mary Jaques, a British traveler to Central Texas in the 1880s, described that the murder of Mexicans, including American citizens of Mexican decent, as something that "carried a sort of immunity with it," and that Mexicans were treated worse than dogs. The lynching of Mexicans, as has been outlined, had become an accepted spectacle, all too often without punishment from the authorities in control. Perhaps the first female Mexican author in the U.S. was María Ruiz de Burton, famous for her 1870s book titled *The Squatter and the Don.* To help bring awareness to such atrocities, she fictionalized the loss of land by Mexicans in California through often violent means and one-sided legalese. She stated, "The Americans must know it; their boasted liberty and equality of rights seem to stop when it meets a Californian… and now we have to beg for what we have the right to demand."

During these years, racial tensions continued as Spanish language documents were removed and disallowed from official government functions, voter suppression of Mexican Americans became commonplace (including charging them a voter poll tax in 1902), further harsh economic disenfranchisement limited educational opportunities, and overall social marginalization persisted. This had been the pattern since 1848 throughout all the ceded Mexican territories and would continue through the 1900s.

ANTI-MEXICAN SENTIMENT HEATS UP

When the secret Zimmermann telegram was intercepted by British intelligence in January 1917, prior to U.S. entry into World War I, its publication enraged Americans and resulted in renewed hate directed at Mexicans in the U.S. The German Foreign office had sent a proposal to Mexico for a military alliance if the U.S. entered the war. In return for Mexico allowing German submarines key port positions, Germany would give generous financial support and eventually help Mexico reconquer the lost territories of Texas, Arizona, and New Mexico. This historic work of intelligence changed world events with the U.S. soon declaring war on Germany and entering WWI. For Mexican Americans, during this time, many examples of mistreatment, blatant abuse and deportations occurred, such as the aforementioned Bisbee affair that forced some 1200

Mexicans to leave the country. Many more examples of such forced repatriations occurred during the early twentieth century. The U.S. expelled some 500,000 Mexicans, 60% of whom were U.S. citizens, during the early years of the Great Depression in the 1930s, including emptying hospitals of sick and disabled Mexican Americans who were grotesquely dumped over the border, some at gunpoint. The state of Colorado in 1936 ordered all Spanish speakers out of the state, the vast majority of which were American citizens of Mexican descent. The U.S. government also denied or discouraged Mexicans from participation in the welfare and charitable programs instituted during the Great Depression created under the Franklin Delano Roosevelt administration. The policies under FDR were atrocious on social and economic issues, and included clear institutional racism against Mexican Americans. Not only did immigration from Mexico to the U.S. practically became non-existent during these years, but many returned to Mexico in search of a better life.

INSTITUTIONAL RACISM

In the 1930s government programs, including the Federal Housing Agency, and commercial banks adopted clear practices of institutional racism that denied Mexican Americans and Black people home and business loans. This permitted cities across the U.S. to start the infamous redlining strategy that affected African American citizens, of which the effects are sadly still evident today. These policies also singled out Mexican Americans by systematically denying them home loans in the more affluent and prosperous blue and green sections of major U.S. cities. This is one of the main factors that has contributed to the current household wealth gap between Caucasians, Latinos, and African Americans. Home ownership has traditionally been one of the main components of attaining the "American Dream." Denying loans and programs to qualified individuals by race and skin pigmentation, as occurred in accordance to the FHA starting in the 1930s, helped to further widen the generational wealth accumulation for Mexican Americans and Black families. Perhaps not surprisingly, white families today have ten times more household wealth than blacks and eight times more than Mexican Americans.

I would like to point out that other factors also contributed to this matter, such as the oppressive societal Jim Crow and Jose Crow segregation, resulting in restricted educational, business, and employment opportunities. This blatant degree of marginalization seen in most communities, especially in the southern U.S. and southwestern states, forced Blacks and Mexicans into poorer inner cities with limited residential, business, and employment opportunities. Institutional and private investments in these inner cities became rare over the following decades, those with means to invest preferring instead to build up suburbs. The mostly white suburbs were simply not available to Mexican and Black minorities. All too often real estate agents were dissuaded, prevented, and potentially fired if caught selling residential properties to minorities in middle and upper class, predominantly white, affluent blue and green areas. In California, there were many instances of actual threats and intimidation. If a Mexican family had happened to "sneak" into one of the more desirable residential areas with better overall infrastructure, including schools, hospitals, shopping, dining, theatres, churches, community sports facilities, and other stores, there would soon appear an anonymous hate letter in their mailbox reminding them in no uncertain terms that they were not only not welcome, but also telling them to go back to Mexico. Little notion was paid to the fact that these residents were more often than not loyal Mexican American citizens, often for generations with little residual connection to Mexico, and in many instances their families had been in the now U.S. territories for centuries. One can only wonder if at any time throughout the southwestern states an Anglo family was rudely told to go back to Europe.

These strategies of systemic racism, specifically redlining, persisted until the signing of the Fair Housing Act in 1968, a follow-up to the Civil Rights Act of 1964. This prevented discrimination concerning the sale, rental, and financing of real estate based on race, nation of origin, gender, religion, handicap, or family status. The memorable passing of the Fair Housing Act was a fitting memorial to the life work and ultimate sacrifice of Dr. Martin Luther King, Jr., and thus passed quickly through Congress after his assassination and prior to his burial in Atlanta. This had been an issue Dr. King highlighted for many years, fighting on behalf of Black and Hispanic veterans returning from Vietnam who were unable to obtain residential and business loans due simply to race and skin color. Senator Edward Brooke, the first African American ever to be elected to the U.S. Senate by popular vote, argued that upon returning from WWII, he had found it impossible to obtain a house loan for his new family because of his race. At least from the standpoint of government-directed institutional racism, the Fair Housing Act officially ended this abhorrent practice.

HOW DO WE PROVE LOYALTY TO THE U.S.?

In the 1940s and 1950s, in addition to the official Jim Crow discrimination against Blacks, anti-Mexican sentiment smoldered. Especially throughout the U.S. southwest and Texas, Anglo Americans still saw Hispanic citizens as unwanted foreigners. The Los Angeles Zoot Suit riots of June 1943 provide a clear example of the racist labeling of Mexicans as a menace to society. White sailors brutally killed such uniquely dressed individuals in the street, then, their thirst for blood not quenched, turned their violent brutal tactics and killing spree on Black people in Los Angeles. After such atrocities, in what Mexican Americans felt would be a watershed moment to finally demonstrate absolute loyalty to the U.S., many seized on the opportunity to enroll in the U.S. armed forces, with somewhere between 250,000 and 500,000 serving their country. The true number is unknown since Hispanics were classified as whites in the armed services. The fact remains that upon returning, instead of being accepted with full citizenship rights of whites, Mexican Americans continued their second-class status, similar to Blacks, with their occupational manual laborer profile unchanged from the pre-war years.

YOUR CHECK IS IN THE MAIL

The now-famous GI Bill of 1944 was intended to help returning war veterans to reintegrate and succeed by providing low-interest home and business loans, educational avenues to obtain valuable trade skills, and enroll in college and university degree programs. However, both Black and Mexican American veterans were largely denied the well-deserved aid by institutional racism inherent in the program. Few obtained loans and only about 5% enrolled in educational programs. Most of these individuals were not aware of the potential benefits they could be eligible to receive. Those that did enroll in training or university programs were insufficiently trained or, due to bureaucratic red tape, tuition checks arrived some five or six months late, forcing them to drop out. I suppose the educational and training checks must have been lost in the mail.

These lending and training gaps between whites and minorities had the predictable effect of creating an income gap. Even when Mexican American veterans managed to obtain a professional degree, their yearly average income was $7,175 versus $8,892 for whites (20% less; an equivalent today of $48,415 versus $60,000). This was also the case for lesser-trained individuals, such as managers and salesmen, with gaps of $1,500 to $2,000 a year. Even untrained day laborers of Mexican decent were paid on average $200 less a year. Sadly, these income gaps remained post Korean War and Vietnam War.

LEGALIZED SLAVERY

The prior waves of Mexican immigration during the Mexican Revolution (1910 to 1929) and the Bracero Program during and after WWII (1942-1964) had ingrained the value of cheap Mexican labor. When WWII caused labor shortages in the U.S., the infamous

Bracero Program was launched in August 1942. By the time the program ended, some four million guest-worker Mexicans had arrived to mostly fill orchards, cotton fields, and ranches in California and the Pacific Northwest and sugar beet farms in the Midwest. Texas opted out of the program, preferring instead to hire farm workers directly from Mexico. Automation decreased labor needs, but not the exploitation and abuses that resulted in the Department of Labor labeling it as "legalized slavery." Subsequently, Mexican immigrants coming to the U.S. looking for work and most Mexican American citizens for the most part accepted this form of racist inequality and were often pushed into performing the most difficult and dangerous jobs since "that's just the way it was" with the gringo boss (a historically derogatory term for racist bosses of Mexican laborer).

An example of these unjust work conditions and hardships experienced by Mexican American workers were the 1902-1903 copper mines protests against the Phelps Dodge Corporation. When workers demanded equal wages as whites, who performed safer and less strenuous tasks and had better work conditions, the protests resulted in the killing and arrests of hundreds of Mexicans. When nothing improved, new protests fifteen years later ended with a similar result. This was and would continue to be the usual pattern. These early 20th century events occurred at about the same time as the previously mentioned forced deportations, stoked by the national publication of the Zimmermann telegram and by President Woodrow Wilson's staunch racism and segregationist ideology, mostly directed at Blacks, yet it did not fail to exacerbate hatred toward Mexicans. There were many other protests in the 1920s by Mexican American workers demanding equal pay and better work conditions with the unfortunate killings and arrests that usually ensued, often with police authorities or the Rangers in Texas and Arizona enforcing the "law" and providing the muscle. Mexican Americans historically had little recourse but to accept these adverse consequences of second-class citizenship.

These historic abuses galvanized WWI veterans in Corpus Christi to form the League of United Latin American Citizens (LULAC) in February 1929, the oldest such organization in the U.S. Its mission has always been to end ethnic discrimination against Latinos in the U.S., while advancing educational, economic, political, healthcare, housing, and civil right agendas that help elevate Latino communities. Their philosophy had been one of assimilation and adaptation to the dominant Anglo-American culture as a strategy to combat racism and discrimination, while improving socio-economic standing. LULAC initially admitted into its ranks only those Latinos who are U.S. citizens and promotes capitalism and individualism as the way to attain the "American Dream." In addition, it adopted English as the official language and promoted that members disavow ties to Mexico, attain formal education, participate politically, and function seamlessly in American institutions.

While newer immigrants have not always embraced the philosophy of total assimilation, preferring to maintain key cultural and religious elements of their nation of origin, the LULAC in the 1960s also moved away from supporting assimilation and, perhaps following the lead of the African American led civil rights movement, started participating in protests to advance Latino causes.

Other post WWII organizations also started fighting for Latino advancement in the U.S., such as the Community Service Organization (CSO) formed in 1948 to increase voter registration and political involvement as well as to desegregate the school system.

The Mexican American Political Association (MAPA) was another such organization which fought to prevent discrimination, encourage political activism, and end school desegregation. The afore mentioned case Mendez et al. vs. Westminster School District in Orange County was upheld on appeal in 1947, finally ending school segregation of Mexican Americans. These organizations also fought against long-standing discrimination in the provision of quality healthcare for Mexicans, Mexican Americans, and other Latinos. The many thousands of returning Mexican American WWII veterans presented an opportunity to decrease the many deficiencies and gaps in the delivery of healthcare services to both veterans and non-veterans. Dr. Héctor P. García, Mexican American veteran, dived deep into this issue.

YOU SAY YOU ARE A VETERAN?

With millions of WWII veterans returning home, the Veterans Administration Hospitals experienced tremendous growth. A hundred thirty-six hospitals were built by 1950. Unfortunately, minority veterans, especially Blacks and Mexican Americans, were systematically denied service connection, and at times determined ineligible for medical services, including mental health services. When admitted to a VA Hospital, minorities often received inferior care compared to whites. It is interesting to note that following the timeline from WWII to the Korean War and finally the Vietnam War, Mexican American veterans became increasingly aware of the various discriminatory practices in the VA Hospital system and more dissatisfied with the medical care received.

To ameliorate the stark situation, Dr. Héctor P. García, also in Corpus Christi, not convinced that LULAC was doing enough to help Mexican American veterans, started the American GI Forum (AGIF) in 1948. The new organization became an effective and powerful advocacy group with multiple national chapters. Dr. García's numerous achievements on behalf of thousands of soldiers, veterans, and their families gradually gained national attention, especially after the much-publicized case of Felix Longoria in 1949 (explained below). Dr. Garcia proved instrumental in obtaining medical care for thousands of Mexican American veterans, especially when it had been insufficient or altogether denied. He also helped families receive war casualties at the airport, even arranging for funeral services. He was noted to say, "It's the least I could do."

NO MEXICANS ALLOWED HERE...EVEN WAR HEROES

In the post WWII McCarthy era, the Justice Department, as part of "Operation Wetback," deported about 700,000 illegal Mexican immigrants. Another 700,000 actual U.S. citizens preferred to return to Mexico for a better life. The dilemma for many Mexicans was based on staying in a hostile country where perhaps an economic advantage could be gained, or returning to a friendly Mexico where their financial status might not be as promising. When the Longoria case became well known, even some war veterans packed up and moved to Mexico, a country where they had never lived.

When private Felix Longoria was killed in action on June 16, 1945, by the Japanese in the Philippines, his young widow Beatrice arranged for his body to be brought back to his hometown of Three Rivers, Texas. When the funeral director refused in 1949 to host a funeral service at the local chapel for him, Beatrice called on AGIF and Dr. García. The case gained immediate notoriety after Dr. García stated that "his Mexican ancestry denied him the dignified burial he deserved." After national protests, then Senator Lyndon B. Johnson arranged for private Longoria to finally rest at Arlington National Cemetery. Dr. García and the AGIF would go on to fight against the post-war racial divide and discrimination facing Latinos, constantly seeking social and political equality as well as equal protection under the law. His organization understood the necessity of political involvement at all levels and joining the burgeoning struggle for civil rights, mostly led by courageous African American leaders, especially James Baldwin and Dr. Martin Luther King, Jr.

NO MEXICANS ON JURIES

Prior to delving into civil rights, let's briefly recall the 1954 case of Pete Hernandez, a Mexican American indicted on murder charges by a white jury in Jackson County, Texas. This case led to the "discovery" that not a single Mexican American had served on a jury for more than twenty-five years. The court learned that there had been a long-standing, county-wide distinction between whites and Mexicans, with voter suppression and segregated schools, until the recent 1947 landmark Mendez case in Orange County. Some restaurants still posted signs stating in no uncertain terms, "No Mexicans Served Here."

The absence of jurors of Mexican descent was the pattern in many counties throughout the southwest, especially in cases involving Mexican Americans. Hernandez vs Texas eventually made it up to the U.S. Supreme Court, which unanimously ruled that Mexican Americans and other cultural groups in the U.S. were entitled to equal protection under the 14th amendment of the U.S. Constitution. The ruling was written by Chief Justice Earl Warren. This was also the first-time lawyers of Mexican descent appeared in front of the U.S. Supreme Court. This case finally opened the legal system in the southwestern states for the first time to selection of Mexican Americans in jury trials, especially when the plaintiff was white and the defendant of Mexican decent.

CIVIL RIGHTS

In the 1960s, a powerful movement called La Raza, formed by Chicano student organizations, brought forth ideologies of Chicano nationalism. Their goals were to fight against discrimination of Mexican Americans that had lasted since 1848, and outline the failures of a culturally pluralistic society. They encouraged Mexicans to instead maintain their own identity and distinctiveness while asserting that "brown is beautiful." The Chicano movement had its roots in the civil rights struggles led by the African American community and was the first to promote Mexican American activism in the U.S. In 1963, in Crystal City, Texas, various groups, including the Teamsters Union and the Political Association of the Spanish-

Speaking Organizations, encouraged Mexican Americans to pay the poll tax and vote for their own candidates in spite of intimidation from the Texas Rangers. When this "revolt" resulted in electoral victory, the story was carried nationally in the New York Times and the Wall Street News, who finally began taking note of America's other minority. Most activists, including the Chicano Movement, focused on immediate issues confronting Mexican Americans, including unequal education, employment opportunities, political exclusion and most interestingly, police brutality. With the novel, global student movements of the late 1960s, the Chicano Movement in 1968 led spontaneous student walk outs in East Los Angeles and Denver, Colorado.

Mexican Americans supported, tagged along, and in some cases joined the fight for civil rights spearheaded by Dr. King. There were additional important contributions such as the United Farm Workers' strike and boycotts aimed at grape growers in California, followed by lettuce workers in California and Arizona, farm workers in Texas, and orange grove workers in Florida.

CÉSAR CHÁVEZ

In 1962, César Chávez and his wife Dolores Huerta founded the National Farm Workers Association (NFWA), instrumental in the support of the 1965-1966 Delano Grape Strike which had been started by the Filipino American farm workers protesting for higher wages. Chávez organized picketers over 400 square miles, prompting police retaliation and an FBI investigation of Chávez and the NFWA. Eventually the United Automobile Workers also supported Chávez, as well as various student non-violent groups (such as SNCC), which helped Chávez and the cause gain national attention. In March of 1966, Senator Robert F. Kennedy attended a U.S. Senate Committee on Labor and Public Welfare meeting in Delano, CA. He met with Chávez, toured a labor camp, and addressed the massive crowd. This meeting generated national and international attention. At the end of 1966, Chávez called for a 300-mile march of penitence, which started with about 300 individuals carrying a Virgin of Guadalupe banner. In the spirit of the Mexican Revolutionary leader Emiliano Zapata, they arrived in Sacramento with some 8,000 individuals, where a weakened, sore-footed Chávez addressed the large crowd.

Over the following two years, Chávez and other supporting organizations led strikes against several core grape growers, eventually earning state-wide, national, and international attention on behalf of workers worldwide. He sometimes implemented Gandhi's fasting tactics with the desired effect. When Senator Kennedy announced his candidacy as the Democratic Party's nominee for the presidency, he asked Chávez to run as a delegate in the California primary. Chávez worked diligently, urging farm workers to support Kennedy, no doubt contributing to his California victory. Chávez attended the Ambassador Hotel victory celebration where Kennedy was assassinated that night. He travelled to New York where he was a pallbearer at the senator's funeral.

Dr. King had been assassinated two months prior. Some in his organization feared Chávez would also be a target. By 1968 Chávez was a national celebrity, so much so that in July 1969 he appeared on the cover of Time magazine. The entire detailed story of the grape growers' strikes, the various organizations, and political maneuverings during those years is a fascinating example of the diligence and persistence of humble workers uniting to achieve major gains. In the end, Chávez and his followers attained most of their goals and on July 29, 1970 when the Delano growers signed contracts with the union in front of the press, agreeing to raise wages, introduce healthcare plans, and provide new safety measures on the use of pesticides

Despite progress in many areas beginning to take place, the Immigration and Nationality Act of 1965, set up quotas on immigrants from Latin counties, especially from Mexico, making seasonal migration between the U.S. and Mexico illegal. This had the effect of millions of illegal immigrants drawn mostly to agricultural areas, often rife with abuse by the employers, simply to make money and return to Mexico without the benefit of workers' rights. This pattern of illegal immigration would persist for the next forty to fifty years and in many ways to the present.

THE GREAT SOCIETY

The U.S. poverty rate in 1964 was 19%. Given a national economic growth of 6% per year from 1963 to 1966, optimism around eradicating poverty loomed large on the Washington political mindset, especially in the White House. President Lyndon B. Johnson had taught poor Mexican Americans some thirty years before at a segregated school in Cotulla, Texas, where he had seen first-hand the pain of prejudice, the lack of opportunity, poverty, and the palpable Mexican American children felt from their white classmates for the simple sin of being Mexican. It was evident that Anglo parents were indoctrinating their children in racist, discriminatory attitudes toward Mexicans. As a younger man, President Johnson had seen this overt prejudice close-up. In 1964, he had also received Daniel P. Moynihan's report on the crisis afflicting Black families, with 25% of children born to unwed mothers. Mr. Moynihan, a sociologist at the Department of Labor, concluded that poverty and urban stress were mainly responsible for this critical situation. In fact, in 1938 African American families had an 11% rate of out of wedlock births and through the 1950s Black women were married at a greater rate than white women. Following the initial civil rights bills passed during the Eisenhower presidency in the late 1950s, and sensing that the time had arrived for "White America to take accountability for the breakdown of the Black family," LBJ promised such intent in a speech at University of Michigan in 1964. He emphatically said, "The challenge of the next half century is whether we have the wisdom to use wealth to enrich and elevate our national life and to advance the quality of our American civilization. For in your time, we have the opportunity to move not only toward the rich society, but upward to the Great Society."

The Great Society was a book written by Graham Wallas in 1914. He was a psychologist and a socialist political scientist, co-founder of the London School of Economics, who suggested that a social-psychological analysis could explain the myriad of social problems as a consequence of the industrial revolution. He compared the role of the environment versus genetics in man. He concluded for humanity to thrive, it should depend on environmental improvements, especially with stronger international cooperation. This must have prompted LBJ to act on the most far-reaching legislative transformation the country had ever seen, outdoing more modest approaches of prior presidents such as Theodore Roosevelt, Woodrow Wilson, and FDR. LBJ's powerful and deft gamesmanship on capitol hill allowed him to continue President John F. Kennedy's initiatives on civil rights laws, adding his own "War on Poverty." In June of 1963, with respect to civil rights, President Kennedy had asked Congress for a bill that would provide "the kind of equality of treatment which we would want for ourselves." Kennedy had experienced for himself the atrocities and rabid racism blatantly directed at Black Americans. I wonder if he also had some concern or even awareness about the historic racist treatment of Mexican Americans in the U.S.

This "War on Poverty" changed the government-citizen relationship forever, to the point of an increased role of government in every facet of daily life and individual decision-making. From then on, a myriad of far-away, unaccountable bureaucrats, emotionally uninvolved and not having lived in nor having spent any time in disadvantaged, struggling communities, would make critical decisions that would have a profound impact in the lives of everyday Americans. Hence the modern welfare state was launched. Sadly, President Ronald Reagan would later comment, "We went to war against poverty, and poverty won."

The stated goals of eradicating poverty and racial discrimination were ironically propelled forward by LBJ, a life-long, rabid, unapologetic racist, who would refer to Black employees as "furniture," among other more egregious, derogatory terms. He even prognosticated, in racist terms, that from then on African Americans would vote Democrat for the next 200 years. His personal feelings about Mexicans were not much better, as it seems he had embraced the ingrained racist and bigoted ideology so prevalent during his Texas youth, even if he had seen such discrimination first-hand. Nevertheless, 1964 to 1968 were remarkable years, a heady time for a myriad of new legislations that gradually welcomed poor minorities into a perpetual state of dependency on big government, still pertinent today. The principal landmark laws included:

1 - The Economic Opportunity Act

2 - The Civil Rights Act

3 - The Elementary and Secondary Education Act and Higher Education Act. The promise was that schools would be shinny and academically sound for everyone.

4 - The Social Security Act. This included Medicare and Medicaid. These two healthcare programs initially enrolled

20 million in Medicare, for those 65 years of age and older as well as the disabled, and Medicaid for the poor initially enrolled 4 million people. Interestingly, by 2020 these have grown to about 62 and 72 million respectively.

5 - The Voting Act

6 - The Immigration and Nationality Act. For the first time, this law removed the long-standing bias favoring European immigrants over all others.

7 - The Department of Housing and Urban Development was started.

8 - The Fair Housing Act of 1968. This officially ended the existing

lending biases, including the appalling practice of redlining, that had existed since the FHA's institutional policies of the 1930s, resulting in the segregation and restriction of opportunities mostly for Black and Mexican minorities, mentioned earlier in this narrative.

9 - Tax cuts. These were instituted from 1963 to 1966 as a result of

the post WWII U.S. boom with GDP growth of 6% per year.

These and other remarkable new legislations, no matter the actual cost that some estimate at fifteen to twenty trillion dollars to date, an amount that could have funded the entire Apollo program sevenfold or more, actually damaged the most vulnerable families and marriages. More than fifty years later, new analyses provide a clearer glimpse into a vision for many in America that was simply wrong and did not translate into stronger families, marriages, and thriving minority communities. The alleged government-guaranteed income to save broken families, especially by incentivizing poor, single mothers to have children out of wedlock, was largely responsible for the break-up of the family nuclear unit and gradually victimized millions of children who instead ended up living in poverty or near poverty in dysfunctional, poor, urban families.

In the America of 1960, according to the U.S. Census Report, some 90% of children were raised in a two-parent family. In fact, in 1938, African American families had two parents at home 89% of the time and in the 1950s Black women were getting married at a higher rate than white women. The Moynihan report of 1965 that sounded the alarm about a "crisis" of 25% of black children being raised by a single parent resulted in the "Great Society" that "officially" married the government to single, poor, black women, while degrading and minimizing the importance of a Black man's critical role in the family and in raising children. Welfare support was (and still is today) for the most part disproportionally denied to poor Black families that had two parents in the home. The Moynihan report did not address Mexican Americans or other Latinos as part of this "crisis," apparently due to the fact that over 90% of Latino families in the 1960s had two parents in the house raising children. Unfortunately, starting in the 1970s, gradually more Hispanic children would be raised by a single parent as well. This new and increasing dependency on government did help some poor families, but it did not come close to eliminating poverty.

> The "War on Poverty" changed the government-citizen relationship forever, to the point of an increased role of government in every facet of daily life and individual decision-making.

In 1966 the poverty rate was similar for Blacks and Hispanics, as it was during the slow economic recovery of 2009-2012, post the 2007-2008 housing and banking crash. A large sector of these minorities took a significant step back through inevitable unemployment, home and business foreclosures, and loss of retirement accounts that followed, destroying their "American Dream."

STAGNANT POVERTY

By 2015, 72% of black children were born to a single mother. By 2017, the rate reached 77%. In 2020, the legacy of the "Great Society" for African American people is one of crime-ridden, burnt-out, bankrupt cities with intergenerational dependence on government welfare programs, and mostly absent of father role models. Perhaps it should be dubbed "The Great Debacle." For African Americans the poverty rate from 1959 to 1969 decreased from 55.1% to 33.2% of the approximate 22.5 million African Americans, whereas the national rate went from 19% in 1964 to 11.2% ten years later. These were remarkable accomplishments in such a short time period. At the same time, poor whites benefited from the welfare state with a significant decrease in the white poverty rate to 7.3% of approximately 172 million people in 1973. These numbers indicate that about 7.5 million African Americans and 12.6 million whites remained in poverty. For the 8.9 million Hispanics recorded in 1970 census, no data are available throughout the 1960s. However, in 1975 the poverty rate was about 28% or about 3 million people. From there the Hispanic poverty rate has mostly tracked the African American rate, hovering from 3-7% lower until about 1995 when the curves crossed over and Hispanics had a higher poverty rate by 1-4%. These rates held mostly in the 28% to 33% range, a pattern of stagnation no different than in the early 1970s. By 2015, the economy improved and the curves crossed again, with a decrease in the Hispanic poverty rate to approximately 20% and that of African Americans settling at about 23%. In 2019, with the economy continuing to grow, the Hispanic poverty rate dropped to 15.7% (~10 million) and African Americans rate to 18.8% (~8 million), the lowest poverty rate for both minorities since 1959. Interestingly, the white poverty rate has remained the same 7.3% from 1973 to 2019 (~17 million). These numbers clearly demonstrate that although gains have been made by both minorities since "The War on Poverty" was launched in the mid-1960s, tremendous inequalities still exist.

	1959/1964	1969	1973/1975	1995	2015	2019
National Poverty	19%		11%	11%		10%
Hispanic Poverty			28%	33%	20%	16%
Black Poverty	55%	33%		28%	23%	19%
White Poverty			7%	7%	8%	7%

WHAT ABOUT THE KIDS?

If one looks at the change in the percent of children under eighteen years of age living in poverty from 2000 to 2013, it increased from 28% to 32% for Hispanics and 31% to 39% for African Americans. By this time, Hispanic children living with two parents had decreased to 57%, trending in the same direction as the African American community. Even more appalling, are the depressing 2013 poverty rates for children living with single mothers: 52% for Latinos and 55% for African Americans. During these years, when President George Bush was in office, 9/11 (2001) occurred and the U.S. involved itself in the costly Middle East "War on Terrorism" in both Afghanistan and then in Iraq, naively believing that these various peoples would soon embrace American style democracy. This time of focus on an active military campaign during the aforementioned subprime loan mortgage housing and banking crises (and subsequent bailout) created a perfect storm for the neglect of minorities most in need. With costs at about one billion dollars or more a month, it doesn't take much imagination to consider how such taxpayer monies could have benefited millions of struggling Americans instead. Insight into these inequalities will be discussed in more detail in the section of this work, titled "Latinos, Education and the Economy."

MR. BALDWIN AND DR. KING DARE DOUBT AND DREAM!

James Baldwin didn't live past 1987 to see the full force of the social program debacle, yet I suspect he may have actually suggested it or even predicted it during the Cambridge Union Hall debate with

Mr. William F. Buckley, Jr., the conservative public intellectual and founder of National Review, when he shared his well-founded doubt and skepticism about what LBJ's the Civil Rights Act of 1964 would actually do for African Americans. Mr. Baldwin, a prolific author and essayist on a variety of themes from sexuality, race, class, and civil rights, was a master orator especially on the entire African American experience in the U.S. He once stated, "It is certain, in any case, that ignorance, allied with power, is the most ferocious enemy justice can have." As it turns out, it's not difficult to imagine that he would be in a state of extreme despair, especially at the current incarceration rate of about 5% of black males forty and older and 7% of those in their thirties. Mr. Baldwin may very well be rolling in his grave. In similar fashion, Dr. Martin Luther King, Jr., in his "I Have a Dream" speech at the Lincoln Memorial in front of a crowd of some 200,000 on August 28, 1963, initially lamented in sobering terms the lack of overall advancement for the Black population in almost every aspect of society since the civil war and the freeing of the slaves. He also, however, ended with high hopes for freedom and equality in America for the African American community. Then on April 3, 1968, he delivered his, "I've Been to the Mountain Top" speech at the Masonic Temple in Memphis Tennessee where he ended by saying: "Like anybody, I would like to live a long life. Longevity has its place. But I'm not concerned about that now. I just want to do God's will. And he's allowed me to go to the mountain. And I've looked over. And I've seen the Promised Land. I may not get there with you. But I want you to know tonight, that we as a people will get to the Promised Land!"

I strongly suspect Dr. King would likewise be at least somewhat dismayed that although from a legal, institutional standpoint equality of opportunity now exists in America, the Promised Land he envisioned, with its "American Dream," for still too many African Americans, Hispanics, Native Americans, and other minorities still remains an elusive dream today.

SUPERIORITY COMPLEX

In almost 250 years since the founding of this young nation, the United States has arguably become the most powerful country in the history of the world, quite an achievement indeed. Those who contest this assertion point to a fatal flaw, a rotten core from the onset, probably understood by the framers, yet conveniently swept aside with the hope that someday a future generation would satisfactorily resolve it and wipe the slate clean. Although a bloody Civil War was fought in the 1860s and a hundred years later civil rights legislation was signed into law, without a doubt both grand accomplishments, the truth remains that the heart of the matter has yet to totally heal. From an Anglo-European perspective, the brand of European racism brought to the Americas which saw all brown, Black, and indigenous peoples as inferior in every aspect, at times as subhuman savages, suited their ideology just fine in creating the "American Experiment" with the white person at the apex. After all, the colonists were intent in risking it all to unshackle themselves from the institutional and religious oppression of an irrational English monarch. However, one must inquire if some of these 17th and 18th century enlightened men pondered for more than a moment any smidgeon of honest self-analysis that would possibly indicate the hypocrisy of their actions, which from our lens more than two centuries later are clearly evident. To be fair, there were a good number of founding fathers who understood the absolute need to abolish the sin of slavery and made their voices heard during those critical early sessions in Congress. Unfortunately, when the economic sustainability of the free-labor dependent southern states was argued, a compromise was reached to table the issue in order to unite and create the new nation.

Is the so called "American Exceptionalism" (defined by the political scientist Seymour Martin Lipset as "the first new nation" with an ideology based on liberty, equality before the law, individual responsibility, republicanism, representative democracy, and laissez-faire economics) at all possible when a significant number of its citizens and residents are enslaved and others treated as second class citizens? Furthermore, the singular sentiment that America has a mission to transform the world and that its very history and mission make it superior to other nations has persisted since its founding. So, can a nation truly be a great nation, especially one claiming such a lofty status in world history, beyond cultural, economic, military, and geopolitical constructs, until the heart beating at the core is healthy, completely cleansed of its original founding sin?

Many would say that from a legal and societal standpoint the U.S. has progressed a long way since 1776 toward this end. That since the Civil Rights Law enacted in 1964, institutional racism has been eliminated with everyone having equal opportunities. Others completely disagree on the grounds that these well-intended laws are not applied evenly on a consistent basis, and that too many people still act in bigoted and racist ways, all too often bending the rules to the detriment of individuals with brown and especially black skin. If one supports the notion that western culture, originating in and brought from Europe to the Americas, has dramatically improved the lives of most human beings on earth and is directly responsible for diminishing worldwide abject poverty by more than 90% since the early 1800s, and has provided all the magnificent and great everyday comforts most of us now take for granted, can western society truly continue to advance and prosper if it does not cleanse itself of the long-existing stain of discrimination?

THE SPANISH TOO

The Spanish Crown and the conquistadores, as we have seen, established in New Spain their own brand of racism, a caste system based purely on skin pigment with their own kind at the top. When indigenous peoples encountered the Spaniards in the Americas, in Mexico, or the southwestern U.S., they were systematically discriminated against, exploited, enslaved, and often killed. Their land and belongings were simply taken from them. To add more tragedy, millions died from the lack of immunity to various European diseases. Some economists today argue that the poverty and economic stagnation still present today in many Latin American countries is at least in part due to the various systems of government imposed by the Spaniards. Many other factors play a role in this issue, but there is probably a grain of truth in this assertion.

These circumstances established the Mexican nation with its hierarchical caste system, finally shed in 1821 when Mexico gained its independence. However, vestiges of this Spanish system of society remain to present times. Sadly, Mexico continues to experience significant discrimination and racism against many of its southern, more rural indigenous populations who have experienced limited opportunities to carve out a living. Over the decades hundreds of thousands of these individuals and families preferred to seek a new life and opportunities in the U.S.

In similar fashion, the southern United States, with the inevitable clash of the Anglo and Mexican cultures, saw similar discrimination and exploitation against Mexican Americans and Native Americans. Thus, it was the European prevailing "superior" western culture, not only the English but also the Spanish, that brought to the Americas a brand of racism that devastated the native populations and enslaved African peoples in the southern United States. Although much progress has been made post emancipation and civil rights, these legacies are still currently at the core of the social issues in the U.S. and in the rest of American continent.

> "It is certain, in any case, that ignorance, allied with power, is the most ferocious enemy justice can have." James Baldwin

THE "ALL MEN ARE CREATED EQUAL" LOOPHOLE

The Declaration of Independence, ratified on July 4, 1776, includes three significant ideas mostly put forth by Thomas Jefferson. These are that (1) people have inalienable rights that include life, liberty, and the pursuit of happiness, (2) that all men are created equal, and (3) the civic duty of individuals to defend these rights for themselves and others. Many consider the second sentence of the Declaration one of the best known in the English language and perhaps, as some have suggested, "the most potent and consequential words in American history." These words, known by many worldwide, have come to emphasize human rights as follows:

"We hold these truths to be self-evident, that all men are created equal, that they are endowed by their Creator with certain unalienable Rights that among these are Life, Liberty, and the pursuit of Happiness."

Awe inspiring indeed! But does it have inherent loopholes? It is my opinion that as altruistic as these words are, there has now come a time to rephrase part of the above statement in the spirit of inclusivity. I shall venture to propose to you, the reader, a variation on the above statement that reads:

"We hold these truths to be self-evident, that all men, women, and children, no matter their race, ethnicity, faith, or sexual orientation, are ALL created equal, that they are endowed by their Creator with certain unalienable Rights that among these are Life, Liberty, the Pursuit of Happiness, and To Live in Harmony with one another."

I'm not certain I will gain any traction or support on making this alteration or amendment, an anathema to many I'm sure, but at the very least the statement to me is far more inclusive than and perhaps excludes the "loopholes" of the original. What do you think? I welcome readers to propose an "improved" version on the above statement. I do expect many critics to say the issue has never been about the original text, that it is perfect as it stands. Instead, they would say the problem has always been the historical application of the concept and laws by flawed individuals, including the slave-owning founders. Any other thoughts? With this in mind, let's move forward to the modern era in our narrative.

THE MODERN ERA 1968-PRESENT

BIRTHDAY DINNER

While enjoying my birthday, home-cooked, gourmet dinner in the fall of 2020 with my two sons, my Italian friend, a gourmet chef, and my girlfriend, the conversation drifted to the protests and riots that had raged across multiple U.S. cities since late May of 2020. My eldest expressed extreme concern about the nature of the Black Lives Matter protests, which claimed to bring attention to police brutality, racial profiling, massive incarceration, and the murder of African Americans. He shared his opinion about what appeared to be senseless destruction of private property and vicious violence aimed at police officers. He emphasized that the killing of innocent people on the streets would not actually accomplish anything productive.

Although he agreed with the message and the need to retrain wayward officers and some police departments, he wasn't for the violence and feared the everyday coverage by the mainstream media had become so politicized that it might actually incite more violence. As he spoke, I could see that my other son was pensive, perhaps feeling uncomfortable. He suddenly blurted out, "Dad, what about the Mexicans? Are they being murdered too? Why don't we hear anything about Mexicans and Latinos?"

I have four children, but two could not join us for dinner since at the time they were living on campus, one at University of Richmond, enrolled in the pre-med program, the other about to graduate with a degree in Political Science from the University of North Texas. I must first admit, I consider myself extremely blessed by any measure anyone may point to. Apart from the fact that my children enjoy great health, as I do as well, they have been born in this country at this time in history — three of them in the mid-1990s and my youngest this century. They have lived in a world that is currently experiencing the most peaceful time in history, the fewest people living in poverty, and readily available technologies that were inconceivable not so long ago. The standard of living and opportunities in the U.S. they have been privileged to take advantage of are beyond what I would consider as truly blessed. At times I have asked myself if that would have been the case if I had stayed in Mexico. What about if I had returned to Canada?

I am a first-generation immigrant to the U.S., having been born in Mexico, initially educated there, attended middle school, high school, and pre-med in Canada, then returned to Mexico for medical school, and finally obtained medical specialty training in the U.S. The pursuit of education has always been a centerpiece of my entire Mexican family, maternal and paternal, with many earning doctorate degrees in a variety of fields including Agricultural Engineering, Cardio-Thoracic surgery, Plastic Surgery, Psychology, Jurisprudence, Chemistry, Business Administration, Accounting, Economics, and various Arts degrees. One of my uncles in Saltillo Coahuila, Mexico, is perhaps the most read columnist in that country. He wrote a highly acclaimed book series titled *The Other History of Mexico*, delving in great detail into the dominant personalities of each era, starting with the war of independence from Spain in 1810. He elegantly manages to present the subject matter and foibles of each character, not only in a delightfully amusing fashion, but also dares to deviate from the "official" history found in school history books. I am more than certain that if he were writing in English, he would have a mantle full of various awards, perhaps even a few Pulitzers, and other such closet-filling trinkets. One of his daily columns is titled "About Politics and Worse." It's about various questionable issues of Mexican politics across the decades, told in a quasi-comical fashion, often highlighting corruption while thanking his "four readers" for their support. At the end of his columns, he once in a while asks a fictitious friend of his, named "Estaca Brown" (approximately translated into English as "That's so wrong" or simply "That's f...d up") to opine about a particular egregious corrupt politician, gross inequity, or such incident or situation. This usually results in concurrently causing the reader to think and to loud laughter. Perhaps when you see something corrupt, unfair, or somewhat questionable, you might too utter "Estaca Brown!" Spanish speakers, especially Mexican Americans, will instantly recognize this remark, and those who don't have my full blessings in appropriating it in your daily lives whenever it suits you.

EDUCATION MATTERS

These picaresque writings aside, the importance of role models should never be understated or underestimated, especially when they are your own family members, not random athletes or movie stars. As I said, I am blessed and extremely fortunate. I have several other key influencers in my life, including my maternal grandfather who arrived from Saltillo, Mexico, to attend Texas A&M University in the mid-1930s to enroll in a master's degree program. Afterward, he returned home to become a leader in his field of expertise, dairy cattle and milk production, both critically needed in a developing nation. My grandfather, aside from his dairy farming endeavors, eventually launched the dehydrated powder milk industry in Mexico with a contraption he called the "Mechanical Cow" which could provide a liter of this protein rich milk for one peso to millions of poor Mexicans. My mother too occupies a special place for her dedication as a lifelong PhD in Psychology conducting clinical research in the difficult area of alcoholism and substance abuse starting in the early 1970s. Her team implemented various, almost unheard of at the time, unique approaches to cognitive behavior modification in the treatment of those afflicted with serious substance abuse. Her program was adopted by substance abuse clinics at Michigan University and in Greenville, North Carolina, as well as by multiple countries such as Norway, Finland, Germany, Spain, Brazil, and Argentina. More importantly for this narrative is that my children, as second-generation Mexican Americans, have chosen to obtain higher education each in different fields. The eldest graduated from Syracuse University with a highly touted five-year degree in Architecture, the next has completed three years at Southern Methodist University where he has been enrolled in the film program, now taking a year off to teach and play competitive tennis, and my younger two as I stated above.

You might say that this is not so unusual for second generations of families that immigrated to this country from Europe, especially Jewish and Anglo peoples, Asians, or those from India. That being the case, to their cultural credit and family diligence, it certainly explains to a large degree the affluence and overall societal success their children and subsequent generations have enjoyed in the U.S. Unfortunately, this has not historically been the pattern for immigrants from Mexico over the last more than 170 years since the end of the Mexican American War in 1848. It definitely points to my rich family legacy as instrumental in the educational paths my children have chosen. The 2019 Latino GDP Report stated that Latino families headed by a college-educated parent has more than double the earnings and four times the net worth of families without a college-educated head of the family. The reality for Mexicans in the U.S. has been mostly the latter. The Public Policy Institute of California reported in 2002 that 69% of Mexican immigrants did not obtain a high school diploma prior to arrival or once in the U.S. Second and third generation Mexican American teenagers did not attain a high school diploma 22% and 20% of the time respectively. According to the National Assessment Educational Program, the Latino high school graduation rate was 60% in 1990 and 85% in 2013. Undoubtedly significant advances have been made, yet Latinos still lag behind African Americans at 92% and whites at 94%. In fact, the high school dropout rate for Latinos decreased from 32% in 1990 to 12% in 2013 and to 10% by 2016. College graduation rates for Latinos from 2010 to 2015 increased by 40%, whereas for non-Latinos rates rose by 13.6%. These figures underscore how far Latinos had lagged behind, but also the effectiveness of new emphasis by Latino families on education as essential for attaining the "American Dream."

In the 2002 report, the age of arrival of Mexicans in the U.S. was a critical factor in whether they attained a high school diploma. Those who came as immigrants between ages fifteen to twenty-one obtained a diploma 28% of the time, while those arriving between ages five and fifteen were at 40%. Lastly, those coming to the U.S. under five years of age obtained a high school diploma 70% of the time. The same report demonstrated family income as the other main factor affecting high school graduation. Interestingly, maternal educational level was a critical factor for African Americans but not for Mexicans. This could perhaps be partly explained by the fact that currently about 60% of Mexican American children grow up in a two-parent family, while only approximately 23% of African American children do. I wonder what "Estaca Brown" would say? It has become clearly evident over the last 30 years that children growing up in two-parent families in the U.S., as measured by every socioeconomic indicator, are far better prepared to succeed in our western society by avoiding a lack of education, pregnancy prior to marriage, creating another generation as a single-parent family, substance abuse, unemployment, and incarceration.

WHAT ABOUT MEXICANS?

These observations point to the fact that my Mexican American children are now better positioned to compete at the highest level in this country, each depending on their own merit. They have not ever been held back by lack of opportunities, never adopted a victimhood mentality, and ultimately been able to attain their own "American Dream." In my family, the regular family time at dinner without phones has encouraged wide-ranging dialogue and discussions. The individuals at the table celebrating my birthday are an amalgam of various ethnicities commonly found among friends in the U.S. My children are one-quarter Chinese since their wonderful maternal grandmother was from Shanghai, one quarter Anglo from their grandfather having mostly from English ancestry, and fifty percent a mix of indigenous Mexican and Spanish blood, who brought to the Americas a splash of African and Arabic DNA. My girlfriend has German and English genetics, while my Sicilian chef friend a delightful mix of Mediterranean genes. From these he inherited a rich legacy of Roman, Greek, Arabic, and North African ancestry, often resulting in his views of America as the inevitable struggle of the powerful versus the weak, the rich versus the poor, the white versus the brown and black, and the English language dominance against the rest. So, for him, the BLM protests are the inevitable consequences of the historically oppressed people finally saying, "No more. The invoice is due."

As we continued to enjoy the sea bass, sautéed vegetables, and shell pasta, with the conversation trending to the concept of equality, my son once again insisted, "Dad, what about the Mexicans? Why is no one talking about police brutality against Latinos, especially against Mexican Americans?" Silence reigned for a few seconds. Undoubtedly, scant few reports have been made about such cases of police brutality against Latinos. A few scattered protests in California did occur earlier in 2020. These were triggered by several killings of young Latinos in California, including 18-year-old Andrés Guardado, shot five times in the back on June 18th, the June 6th shooting of twenty-three-year-old Erik Salgado and his pregnant girlfriend, resulting in his death and that of the child, and on June 2, twenty-two-year-old Sean Monterrosa, shot five times through the windshield by an officer in an unmarked police vehicle. These incidents ignited some local, brief protests, but minimal national attention about historic violence and brutality against Latinos in the U.S. One could say it was almost ignored by the mainstream media. My son, upset, asked, "What if these young individuals had been Black?"

We looked up several published sources online. The Washington Post database reporting such statistics since 2015 to the present, shows nearly 1,000 Latinos had been killed by the police in the U.S.

According to the Los Angeles Times, 465 Latino individuals were shot and killed in L.A. County alone since 2000. Since a breakdown of the different Latinos is not provided, I would guess the vast majority were of Mexican descent (since 90% of Latinos in California are Mexican). Needless to say, we were taken aback, especially since the Washington Post database on individuals shot by police from 2015 to 2019 reported a total of 5740 such killings, 95% men and more than half of the victims ages 20 to 40. The total number of Blacks killed was 1,352, whites 2,600, and Latinos 949. When adjusting for population, Blacks were killed at a rate of thirty-two per million, whites at thirteen per million and Latinos at twenty-four per million. In 2019, according to this database, there were fifty-five unarmed people shot and killed by the police. Fourteen were black and twenty-five white men. The number of Latinos was not specified. We also noted that in 2016 there were 144 African American individuals killed by the police in the U.S. and in the same year there were also 94 Latinos killed, yet most these lost lives received little to no national attention by the mainstream media. This directly points to the ongoing national neglect of Latino victims.

My oldest son, almost outraged, asked a series of questions: "Why do so many people get upset when someone says All Lives Matter? I don't get it. Latinos are getting killed too! Don't Mexican lives matter? Aren't we important in the U.S?"

My other son pitched in. "Dad, I think they only want us Mexicans for the hard work it takes to build this country, to serve in the military, and for us to just shut up, pay taxes, and stay invisible!"

As these questions hung in the air, my Italian friend added,

"Most people in this country don't know the history of Mexicans in the U.S. Even the politicians get Latinos riled up about racism every four years just to get their vote, and what little they know is mostly a negative perception."

With those thoughts in mind everyone was served a generous slice of coconut birthday cake and a small mountain of rocky road ice cream as "Las Mananitas," the beautiful traditional Mexican birthday song, was sung in my honor. While relaxing after dessert, my eldest son asked, "Dad why don't you tell us about who we are, you know, the Mexicans?"

Dr. Maese's children

Dr. Maese providing medical info in Spanish on a pandemic hotline

More and more Mexicans graduate high school, go to college, and attain 4-year degrees every year.

Dr. Maese's friend and podcaster

 Successful Mexican H[illegible] specialist.   Mexican billing & collections specialist.

Mexican entrepreneur

Mexican Art Gallery

Mexican-
Owned
Businesses

Mexican American owned businesses

Traditional Mexican Dancers

Alvaro Munoz, Director of Ballet & his dance partner

Young Mexican ladies proud of their heritage

Traditional Mariachi dancers

LATINOS AND THE MEDIA

The mainstream media's considerable role in providing information 24/7 gives it the ability to influence large swaths of the U.S. population, positively or negatively, about a particular individual or group. For several decades, these English language media networks have neglected, marginalized, or reinforced negative racial stereotypes and biases about Mexicans and Latinos, at times amplifying and overestimating local and national level fears about Latino criminality. The absence of Latinos in journalistic institutions such as liberal publications that include the New York Times and the Washington Post, have had just one Latino on their editorial boards. These "top elite journalistic" publications have actually marginalized and at times erased Latino voices.

A Washington Post study that analyzed publications from 1996 to 2016, including 185,000 articles in local, regional, and national papers and magazines, revealed that about two-thirds of all articles pertaining to Mexicans and other Latinos were negative. About 37% of these articles focused on criminality, 21% on topics relating to economic threat to the U.S. (unemployment, poverty, and welfare), and 12% on illegal immigration. Only one in four articles focused on positive topics such as culture and achievement. From 2008 to 2014, the English language mainstream media national evening news programs (CNN, NBC, CBS, and ABC) spent a mere 0.78% of their on-air time on Latino issues, or about 87 seconds per evening. Furthermore, just like print media, two-thirds of this coverage was of a negative nature, once again focusing on criminal activity and illegal immigration.

Not unexpectedly, this poor track record and an almost total absence of coverage highlight the perception that Latinos do not matter, except every four years during presidential elections. Politicians feed Latinos the usual racist narratives flung by one political party against the other and the "you are oppressed and therefore a victim" label and the "we care about you" tag lines. We Latinos are not stupid.

Over the last twenty years the media has certainly become more subjective opinion than objective journalism, how they cover different people and issues being dependent on the corporations that own each network or publication and which political party they align with. We are currently in a sad state of affairs, as the most recent elections have demonstrated. When a reporter actually wants to publish a piece, he or she first encounters editorial censorship to ensure the article lines up with the established company's and network's political alignment. This may be the main reason that two-thirds of Latinos and three-quarters of Blacks feel that the mainstream media and social media networks and platforms do not understand them, and have not fulfilled their promises of not only more coverage, but more accurate and fair coverage of their people and other underserved ethnic communities.

Today, it is imperative we understand that about two-thirds of all U.S. adults are online, have smart phones, and have more options than ever to obtain information from a variety of sites, ranging from the extreme left to the extreme right. If manipulation and clever, underhanded censorship occurs, especially by legally immune web platforms sometimes now functioning as publishers, with people steered like sheep in a certain direction, then the eventual result will be a catastrophic, Orwellian-style dystopia. When Spanish language networks have a parent company with a one-sided bias, Latinos can be manipulated along a certain narrative. What will happen when all the networks toe the party line in unison? What are Latinos to think about this? How do Latinos that just want to work and care for their families fit in all of this polarized mess? Who do they trust and believe? Do Mexicans and Latinos even matter? Or are we just an afterthought and should quietly just do the hard manual labor, fight for the country when called, pay taxes, and not complain?

JAMES BALDWIN... WHAT CAN WE LEARN?

In 1965 a debate was held at Cambridge Union, Cambridge

University, between James Baldwin and William F. Buckley, Jr., the editor of the conservative right-wing magazine "National Review," as mentioned previously. The debate asked: "Has the American Dream been achieved at the expense of the American Blacks?" Mr. Baldwin, an internationally recognized novelist for his writings and conferences on the plight of the African American population, eloquently and in great detail made his case for the historical complete disenfranchisement for almost 400 years of the Black population in the U.S. He emphasized not only the consistently denied societal opportunities to attain their own "American Dream," but that this long-standing pervasive inequality has actually hindered such attainment by the Black population. He warned about the future American society, that unless this grave situation were to be reversed by eliminating systematic racism in the laws of the land and their implementation in the real everyday world, this oppressed, frustrated minority, perhaps through rebellion, would eventually wreck it.

The despair in his words was evident as he recounted that the abolishment of slavery a hundred years before did not come close to helping African Americans attain actual freedom, nor did it narrow societal, financial, and legal inequality under the law. Therefore, he doubted the civil right bills, recently signed by the Johnson administration, would have the desired impact on improving the overall status of African Americans. Mr. Buckley, for his part, argued that the Black problem in the U.S. was a complex issue, one not easily solved, and created by the unfortunate collision of two factors. On the one hand, there is the historical importation to America of the European deeply engrained sense of racial superiority resulting in the not-too-subtle forceful efforts to spread discrimination and racism against the Black population. The second factor, weighing against the first, was what he felt were insufficient sacrifices and efforts of said minority to improve and advance their own lot. He stressed that Blacks also needed to be held accountable for their situation.

The notion that "The American Dream was achieved at the expense of American Blacks" was approved by the student body present that day at Cambridge Union with 544 for to 164 against. These undergraduate English students seemed to grasp that the ideals of the American experiment had failed one-ninth of its population. At no moment in the eloquent debate did anyone ponder the possibility that at least in some way Mexicans in the U.S. had perhaps also been excluded from attaining such a dream. Could one consider that the American Constitution, in all its magnificence and declaration that all men are created equal, had simultaneously failed the Mexicans?

Fast forward to 2020, a year that will forever be marked throughout the world as paradigm changing by virtue of the collective determination by most ethnic groups to take a stand and dramatically change society at large. The worldwide coronavirus pandemic and widespread protests against police brutality and inequality affecting Black people, with willing participation by individuals of all races, including whites, undoubtedly marked 2020 as a turning point in world history. Much remains to be played out on these complex social matters since the curtain has been pulled back yet again, although it's unfortunate that the dialogue has become highly politicized and at times violent.

One of the 2020 presidential election "surprises" was the fact vast numbers of minorities shifted their vote away from their traditional Democratic Party candidates, probably indicating their antipathy for socialism and defunding the police mandates. But there was something else. Current polling shows a continuation of this trend, perhaps because minorities are no longer blind to the four-year cycles of cheap pandering and the promises of more welfare programs that historically result in greater dependency on government and ultimate borderline poverty.

These minorities do not want to be identified by the color of their skin as oppressed victims, relying on a government entitlement programs, but rather the opposite: as Americans, intellectually capable and hard-working, more than able to support themselves while contributing to society at large and thus gaining dignity and confidence along that journey. After much suffering in 2020, with a new administration in Washington plus the COVID-19 pandemic mostly behind us, one cannot but sit back and contemplate all the issues that occurred in 2021 and thus far in 2022. The world has become much more complicated. The exit from Afghanistan resulted in the tragic death of thirteen service men and women, five of them Latinos, after a suicide bomber at the Kabul airport self-detonated. This was an avoidable catastrophe.

Widespread school lockdowns on account of the pandemic predominately affected millions of public-school children who fell further behind on their academics while this strategy imposed by public health officials significantly augmented diseases of despair and domestic abuse. In retrospect, given the extremely low risk for serious disease from covid-19, the imposed lockdowns on young people were a mistake. Then of course, there is the worst inflation and gas prices seen in decades that affects most Americans, but in particular minorities and economically disadvantaged whites. To some degree these issues were made worse by the Russian invasion of Ukraine in February of 2022 and the supply chain crisis that ensued, but the non-gaslighting reality is that many of the government policies adopted since early 2021 have resulted in this current catastrophic situation. The printing of trillions of dollars that have been pumped into the economy, plus a war on fossil fuels, and an open border policy that has allowed more than two million undocumented immigrants, most unvetted, and the unprecedented entry of illegal lethal drugs, will surely have a tremendously negative impact on the economic wellbeing of most Americans by further stressing the educational, welfare, criminal, and healthcare systems. The most affected will be minorities, who will likely absorb into their communities most of these newcomers. Mexican Americans have been seriously impacted by all these issues.

Furthermore, these conservative Mexican Americans and other Latinos, many of them parents to children in the public school system, are now further stressed and conflicted by the introduction of radical gender and race ideologies completely foreign and contrary to their traditional cultural and religious values. Recent proposals and laws for more massive spending by the federal government are predicted by various think tanks and by the congressional budget office to result in more overall hardship for most small business owners and middle- and lower-income people in the U.S. Given the myriad of current issues, Mexican Americans, other Latinos, and

Blacks are in for a rough journey for the foreseeable future. Upcoming elections will likely reflect the general disconnect and discontent by Mexican Americans and other Latinos with the current policies. One may reasonably ask if these groups were taken into consideration by lawmakers when instituting and imposing such policies. We as a country are facing a complicated, and rapidly changing world indeed.

THE NEGLECTED MINORITY

We often see and hear people discussing impacts of various policies on Blacks, but what about Mexican Americans and other Latinos? Little is said in the mainstream media about the plight of the largest minority in the U.S. Latinos make up approximately 18.5 % of the entire population, two-thirds of which are of Mexican descent. Protests by groups such as BLM across the country focus on police brutality and inequities adversely affecting African Americans, yet such notions are rarely applied to Latin peoples, who have often had similar adversities and at times even worse. The media rarely or never talk about the history of Spanish-speaking peoples in the U.S., especially that of Mexicans.

The historical record is undebatable on the presence of Mexicans in North America, including the current southwestern states, long before the Anglo populations arrived. To that effect, could someone today at the Union Cambridge debate hall reasonably ask: "Has the American Dream been achieved at the expense of Mexican Americans?" I can just wonder who these enlightened Cambridge Union students would invite to debate in favor of the proposition. Is there a Mexican version of a James Baldwin or someone like him in our midst? On the other hand, we may count on a large number of William Buckley-like figures to take the opposing debate position and in similar fashion assert that Mexican Americans, although historically targets of Anglo-European racism and injustice, are themselves culpable for largely remaining on the fringes of that "American Dream," mostly on account of their poor adherence from generation to generation to the principle that education is the great equalizer and the ultimate gateway to attaining the "American Dream." Or should Latinos believe the distinguished Tom Brokaw, retired long-time national news anchor, who stated, "Latinos need to work harder on assimilation"? Perhaps we should forgive Mr. Brokaw for his simple, shortsighted analysis, possibly an easy conclusion coming from a platform of privilege and traditional elitism, never having had to reach down to the bucket of brown lives to mingle with and understand them.

With the current reality of Latino high school dropout rates of one and a half times that of African American students and double that of whites, the coming generations of Latinos, especially in the era of reliance on social media, advancing technologies, and increasing automation, may well continue to lag even further behind. Is there a historical basis for this unfortunate phenomenon? According to The Joint Economic Committee, the current median net worth of Hispanic households, including Mexican Americans, is about one-eighth that of whites. The median household income is about $20,000 less than whites. This causes me to wonder where these parameters will be in 2060 when Hispanics will make up nearly a quarter of the U.S.

population.

SMOLDERING RACISM

The Latino population has exploded in the U.S. from 8.9 million in 1970 to about 60 million in 2020, or from about 4.4% to 18% of the total U.S. population. This can be attributed to various migration waves from Mexico, Central America, and to a lesser extent from South America. Puerto Ricans and Cubans have resided in the U.S. for well over a hundred years as well, mostly concentrated in New York and Florida. The higher birth rate of Latinos compared to other racial groups has also contributed to this explosion.

Since the late 1960s and well into the 1990s, an anti-Mexican sentiment has continued to smolder, especially in the southwestern United States. Do you remember the beginning of this book where I talked about never having suffered from racism in the U.S.? An issue many people have is not being able to simultaneously acknowledge the vast history of racism in America and the great progress that has been made. Too often, people have trouble accepting that there are lots of people who have not experienced the negative effects of racism while at the same time lots of people have. We must be able to hold these thoughts in our minds concurrently to take an honest look at racism, prejudice, and bias logically instead of emotionally. And then evaluate what else needs to change. That is why I have and will continue to include facts that are often unknown, unrecognized, and sometimes ignored. What is the saying? You must first acknowledge a problem before you can fix it. Racism has historically been a huge problem in the U.S. It is still a problem, but has diminished greatly.

However, despite the changes and enormous progress already made, many of the impacts remain. That is why we're delving into Hispanic and, specifically, Mexican American history. And why I feel obligated to highlight what has been mostly overlooked.

Many instances of brutality against Mexicans have occurred throughout the history of the U.S. Some we covered in previous sections, but those transpired in the more distant past. Others, such as the 1976 Douglas, Arizona, case against George Hanigan and his two sons who tortured and burnt the feet of three agricultural laborers just for crossing their ranch, happened in more recent times. After the Mexican government filed a complaint, one of the sons was actually found guilty and served time in prison, one of the first such instances. Since the 1980s Mexican immigrants and other Latinos have moved to the U.S. in droves, mostly seeking work due to the Latin American debt crisis and multiple devaluations that resulted in high unemployment and destruction of large portions of middle-class savings. The Immigration Reform and Control Act of 1986 granted amnesty to illegal immigrants who had lived in the U.S. before 1982 and imposed penalties on employers hiring illegal immigrants, who skirted the law by hiring workers from subcontractors who took full advantage by taking a generous cut from the workers' wages. Now I say, "Estaca Brown!"

A 2015 study reported that the legalization of some three million immigrants resulted in a decrease in property crime of about 3-5%. Conversely, a 2018 study in the American Economic Journal found that restricting employment opportunities for unauthorized migrants resulted in higher crime rates. This law paradoxically resulted in an increase from five million illegal immigrants in 1986 to just over eleven million in 2013. Some claim that by 2020 there were in excess of twenty million illegal immigrants in the U.S., hence it's worthwhile considering what is the best policy moving forward regarding amnesty programs and work visas. Perhaps the lessons from 1986 can serve to guide policy makers today in this regard. What I can definitely confirm is that for Mexican Americans already living in the U.S., especially in the southern border states, a legal immigration policy is their preference and not the current dangerous and intrusive open border we are experiencing daily. The idea by some policymakers that Spanish speaking people from different countries all get along just because they speak the same language is erroneous and completely shortsighted. As mentioned above, the illegal migrants will more likely than not end up living in neighborhoods with Mexican Americans and Blacks in an uneasy and potentially dangerous relationship that will augment crime, overcrowd schools, and increase competition for jobs. It is predictable that an open border policy will be rejected by Mexican Americans and most Latinos at the polls.

The 1994 economic debacle and the Mexican Peso Crisis at the end of the Salinas Presidency resulted in significant distress and brought more migrants to the U.S. The NAFTA trade agreement, together with the prior 1991 elimination of small landowners that had existed since the end of the Mexican Revolution in 1929, brought hundreds of thousands to urban centers looking for work. Many of these people eventually migrated north of the border after U.S. corn subsidies brought down grain prices and worsening widespread government corruption, both contributing to the crash of the Mexican economy and skyrocketing unemployment. As mostly poorly educated Mexicans and other Latinos rushed into states like California, discrimination escalated. California voters widely approved proposition 187, making healthcare (except in an emergency), public social services, and public education all unavailable to illegal immigrants. Mexican Americans reacted by protesting that the proposition was reminiscent of pre-civil rights era ethnic discrimination, eventually being deemed unconstitutional by the Ninth Circuit court in San Francisco. The Chandler Roundup of 1997 in Chandler, Arizona, was another example of anti-Mexican sentiment that resulted in the arrest, based solely on skin color, of individuals suspected of being illegal immigrants, including many citizens. Many more such instances exist that have for the most part received little to no media coverage, a pattern that remains to date, as noted previously in the section "Latinos and the Media."

NEW CENTURY

The 2000 U.S. Census showed that Mexican immigrants accounted for 43% of the 11.3 million foreign-born immigrants. Most of these new immigrants found work throughout the U.S. in agriculture, construction, textile mills, chicken processing, and as day laborers. The Latino population searching for work rapidly increased by three hundred to four hundred percent in states such as in Georgia, North and South Carolina, and Arkansas. From time to time this resulted in violent clashes with local whites, and overt discrimination mostly in places that had not yet been accustomed to the Latino presence. In the years after 9/11, Mexican and other Latin illegal immigrants stayed on the U.S. side, avoiding the tighter security at the border, and preferring to just send money home every month. They moved away from seasonal agricultural jobs to more permanent year-round employment in restaurants, construction, landscaping, hotels, and factories. The problem was that most paid social security taxes into fake accounts so they were not eligible for benefits, and too few paid federal or state income tax since their wages were low. Interestingly, the Earnings Suspense File, which is used to track social security numbers that do not match government records, grew by an average of 67 billion dollars per year from 2000 to 2007. It would appear that the windfall from these economic refugees, who did not receive benefits, contributed significantly to the social security system. Most analyses demonstrate that undocumented immigrants contribute more than they take in payments, as was the case in Texas in 2006 with $1.58 billion produced by such individuals versus $1.16 billion paid out in state services. To be fair, these individuals also paid sales tax on purchases and property taxes via rents to landlords. By 2007 there were some twelve million undocumented workers in the U.S. as a result of 9/11 border policies and poor economies in Mexico and Central American countries that kept the flow mostly in a northern direction. In the 1994 poorly executed, low-budget, satiric film by Director Sergio Arau, "A Day without a Mexican," the California Dream and the economy comes to a halt due to the mysterious disappearance of Mexicans who perform most of the daily manual labor. Comedy or not, Latino people have become the labor backbone of the U.S., contributing to every sector of the U.S economy so much so that if all American Latinos were a country according to the 2017 Latino GDP Report, it would be the seventh richest country in the world, well ahead of Canada, England, Italy, and Brazil, and the third fastest growing just behind China and India.

LATINO DIVERSITY

In contrast to the above statistics, the U.S. African American population in 1970 was 22.5 million and in 2020 about 42 million, or approximately 11% and 13% respectively. There are also increasing numbers of Afro-Latinos and Afro-Caribbean individuals. According to a 2014 Pew Research Center survey, one in four U.S. Latinos identify as Afro-Latinos, definitely an increasing population of people. As we explored in the first section, Mexicans have on average 5% of their DNA from African ancestry and many more from Central American nations such as Guatemala and Caribbean islands such as the Dominican Republic have significantly more Black ancestry. In reality, according to the Slaves Voyages website, of the 10.7 million Africans taken to the New World, some 388,000 landed in what became the U.S., 200,000 more taken to Mexico and 4.86 million to Brazil. The other five million were taken to the various Caribbean islands, some of them referred to as the sugar islands. There were an additional 52,000 people brought to the U.S. via internal routes in the Americas. Latino individuals identifying as Black have also experienced a long history of racial discrimination hierarchies brought to the Americans by the Europeans. They often find themselves having to correct the misperception that racism has been solely a U.S. issue, when in fact the stain of racism has existed and continues to exist well beyond its borders. (In fact, while racism based on pigmentation has been the dominant form of racism for several hundred years, almost every culture throughout the history of the world has had some form of rampant discrimination.)

These diverse Latino peoples each have their own identity and culture, but are all too often lumped together by Anglo Americans and other Europeans. Even though about two-thirds of all Latinos are of Mexican descent, one should not assume that a particular Latino is Mexican just because that individual speaks Spanish, a frequent pet peeve of many non-Mexican Latinos. Just as English speakers may have different countries of origin, different linguistics, customs, and cultures, so obviously do Latinos. The currently observed diversity of the Latino population in the U.S. is the result of the increased migration from South and Central America mainly over the last thirty years.

CENTRAL AMERICAN TRAGEDY

A close Puerto Rican friend, who lived for some years in Miami, recently made an interesting comment to me. He said Miami residents could tell which Central or South American or Caribbean dictator or strongman was oppressing his people by the number of immigrants suddenly arriving in Miami from that country. Historically, this situation represents a longstanding humanitarian catastrophe. These immigrants and their families seeking political or economic refugee status or asylum include those escaping from various regimes such as those of Nicaraguan Dictator Anastasio Somoza, Paraguayan Dictator Alfredo Stroessner, Panamanian Dictator Manuel Antonio Noriega, Chilean Military Dictator Augusto Pinochet, Cuban Dictator Fidel Castro, and more recently Venezuelan Dictators Hugo Chávez and Nicolás Maduro. It has not been my purposeful intent to omit any other dictators or strongmen, so I apologize in advance if I have been remiss on mentioning you on the illustrious list of those who have somehow maligned their compatriots.

Perhaps one can add that the U.S. has gained from these individuals, who in most cases bravely risked it all as they embarked on an uncertain journey to provide for their families a better, more prosperous life.

Migration from Central American countries to the U.S. dates back to the early 1980s, when civil wars in El Salvador, Guatemala, and Nicaragua started various waves of immigrants heading north. Even after peace agreements were signed, widespread poverty, unemployment, and corruption remained, pushing people to migrate north. In some cases, natural disasters such as the devastation caused by Hurricane Mitch in Honduras in 1988 drove migrants to the U.S. Another factor is the surge caused by the prevalent drug trafficking, violence, and high homicide rates which have ramped up since the early 1990s. The current strategy since 2015 of providing some $750 billion a year to Central American countries to correct the issues on the ground, with some claiming much of these funds are stolen by corrupt officials in the recipient countries, while the significantly lesser amount of $20 billion a year is spent on enforcing the law at the U.S. border. Till this situation is corrected to help the local economies and law enforcement efforts, as well as sponsorship programs for children, the number of asylum seekers will continue to grow. The fact is that Mexican migration has been on the decline since 2009, while Central American migration is on the rise.

LATINOS AND THE MAINSTREAM MEDIA

The current status of the relationship of the mainstream media and the U.S. electorate has a rather peculiar history dating back to the President Clinton administration in the 1990s. When Fox News devised a strategy to talk to conservatives and the right-leaning segment of the U.S. population with predominantly negative stories about Democrats, especially President Clinton, the Clinton Foundation, and the associated sex and money scandals, their daily subscribers and profits grew exponentially. It was the end of genuine fair and more balanced journalism. Even if traditionally the mainstream media had a subtle long-standing liberal democratic party bias, this change ushered the launching of a new era of stark bi-partisan reporting that created polarization in the country, mostly along party lines. It was the beginning of corporate opinion masquerading as news, all at the same time. In subsequent years, during President George Bush's administration, post 9/11, other competing networks soon realized that it would be a wise business decision to take an opposing position and mainly target liberals and the left-leaning public. This profit motive created an entrenched ideological battleground that resulted in a Grand Canyon-sized media divide that continued to widen during the President Obama administration. Never had a president been regarded by most of the mainstream media as the omnipresent and omniscient messiah! The "no scandal administration" moniker applied to the Obama presidency was and continues to be fiction.

When President Trump arrived on the scene, what had been a Grand Canyon-wide divide between the few conservatives and right-leaning versus the majority of liberal, left-leaning news networks, the rift became wider than both the Atlantic and Pacific Oceans, with each network speaking mainly to their base. Content long ago had ceased to be news, becoming just offensive opinion pieces not unlike the torpedoes that sank the U.S. fleet at Pearl Harbor. If someone wanted to work for these networks, then as a good soldier their opinion pieces must adhere strictly to the corporate ideology or they'd risk losing their job and possibly career. President Trump, a novice politician whose personality and delivery are all too easy to ridicule and critique, came into a bullfighting ring armed with a feeble red cape to face a multitude of fired-up angry bulls. The mainstream media and the democrats waged all-out war even before the 2016 election had really begun.

This relentless marathon-like, adversarial, political, and mainstream news campaign, with a win-at-any cost, full court-press attitude, indeed prototypically Machiavellian, has not taken a breather even after President Biden's inauguration and first years in office. Now that the new Obama-like administration is in power, the anointed unification messiah sitting in the White House has not yet been able to accomplish the promised cooling of the national temperature and unification of the country, but perhaps the opposite. Our sincere wish and hope, as everyday citizens, is that President Biden succeeds in these lofty endeavors. Certainly, the mainstream media's incessant attack and defend opinion positions, in favor of or against the other political party and its members, will have to be cooled, perhaps even calling a truce. Otherwise, viewers will continue to be fed one-sided, biased information that results in further divisionism. Unfortunately, for Mexican Americans and other Latinos who consume Spanish-language news networks, all too often these are controlled by the same corporate media, such as in the case of Comcast and Telemundo, creating a single, biased narrative that clearly attempts to manipulate opinion. We must all guard against such manipulations and search for ourselves to obtain more balanced information.

This gamesmanship has also extended to social media platforms, who have clearly become biased publishers during the last few years. They have entered the fray with obvious partisan fact checkers subjectively censoring opposing voices in detriment of free speech and freedom, while protecting their preferred candidate and party. One must also not forget the role of the once great print newspapers such as the Washington Post and New York Times, among others, who are barricaded behind left-leaning opinions, frequently to extreme levels, and lecturing daily against conservatives and of course President Trump. Recent Pulitzers awarded to such publications have never been so degraded. If the goal has been to only speak to a homogeneous population of like-minded subscribers who can only stomach one-sided attacks and are not willing to try to understand or dialogue with those holding a different opinion or point of view, and instead labeling them as racist, xenophobic, or some other derogatory term, then these publications have succeeded. The media has in fact been culprit and complicit in proving that famous Lincoln saying: "A house divided against itself cannot stand." During these sad times of extreme political polarization, multiple independent outlets and podcasters have quickly emerged and flourished by providing substance and a balanced, free-speech approach that I suspect, over the coming years, will continue to draw a larger and larger audience away from the mainstream media and some social media platforms.

The summary of the current state of the mainstream media and online platforms, publications, and periodicals is an almost complete loss of credibility and trust. So how does this affect Latinos?

The sad truth is that the mainstream media, with few exceptions, still thinks of Latinos as a monolith that can be manipulated, especially around election time, which almost completely ignores the diversity and complexity of Latino voters. This implies that the English language media's opinion is that Latinos lack sophistication and intelligence. Comcast owns NBC and Telemundo, both mostly reporting pro-left-sided political bias as per the main corporation's orders. Univision, recently purchased by two companies controlled by Wade Davis, has traditionally had pro-left-leaning reporting, mostly pro-Democrat, at times feeling more like activism and leftist propaganda masquerading as news. The Trump era galvanized even more racist rhetoric aimed at all Republicans and conservatives, most of it unwarranted, in order to control Latino opinion and vote. Will that change in the near future under the new leadership?

These networks and presidential candidates would be wise to consider how Latinos voted in the 2020 presidential election. According to sources at CNN, CNBC, NBC, and the New York Times, in the five states where Latinos make up at least 20% of the vote (Arizona, Florida, California, Nevada and Texas), Biden led Trump by 19% among Latino men and by 33% among Latinas. Specifically, in California Biden won 76% of the Latino vote and 79% of the Latina vote. In contrast, Florida showed more even numbers at 51% for Latinos and 53% for Latinas, both in favor of Biden. In Texas the numbers were 55% and 61% for Latinos and Latinas respectively, both in favor of Biden. While in California, Texas, and Arizona the vast majority of Latinos are Mexican Americans, in Florida, Cuban Americans make up 6% of all Florida voters and Puerto Ricans 5%. A new contingency of Venezuelan voters also made their voice heard in Florida, with a clear message of most of these Latinos rejecting a socialist agenda in view of the historic atrocities in Cuba by the Castro dictatorship, and the more recent debacle in Venezuela. In summary, an analysis of the votes cast in thirteen states, Latinos supported Biden on average by a margin of 2:1. Overall, Latinos cast 16.6 million votes in 2020, an increase of 30.9 % over the 2016 presidential election. By comparison, turnout was 15.9% higher among voters of all races. This dramatic increase in Latino participation will likely continue to rise, especially with its rapidly expanding, adult, voter-eligible population, making the overall Latino vote a swing electorate in future elections. The millions of Latinos that helped the Biden-Harris ticket expected their needs to be reflected in federal policy.

Unfortunately, almost two years into the administration, with very few examples, this cannot be said to have come to fruition. Even the messaging has been poorly received. Just using the term Latinx, as many politicians and the mainstream media continue to promote, has been poorly accepted by the vast majority of Latinos and Latinas, who are highly protective of their native language and traditional gender roles, and view these as vital to their cultural values. This neologism in American English, first appeared online in 2004, then in 2013 in a Puerto Rican psychology journal challenging traditional gender binaries in the Spanish language, has been incorporated by only 2-3% of Latino people and almost no one over age of fifty (most of the Latino voters!). The term is exclusively used in the U.S., all too often by pandering left-leaning politicians who simply do not understand that it is highly unpopular among Latinos and Latinas! This transparent attempt, by anglophones, at diversifying the Spanish language for the purpose of inclusivity is unnecessary since the Latino people living in the U.S. already readily accept and embrace the LGBT+ community. Another important political and social messaging issue is that of Critical Race Theory or CRT. Attempts in some school districts to incorporate CRT into educational curriculums has been met with strong opposition. While acknowledging and studying the historical sins and atrocities against various minorities, as has been outlined in the previous chapters of this book as it pertains to Mexican Americas, is vital to understand a better path forward, simply boiling down all U.S. financial, government, and educational institutions, and all white people as inherently racist is wrong. Teaching minority children, or anyone else for that matter, that racism is baked into every aspect of daily life, and into every institution, is anathema to what Latinos currently believe. In essence, judging people by the color of their skin, and not the content of their character, is morally abhorrent and completely opposed to the Judeo-Christian values most Latinos hold dear. Holding white people today accountable for the sins of some of their ancestors is wrong. If CRT simply teaches factual history with the purpose of learning so that we may all benefit by avoiding past horrors, then welcome; otherwise Latinos will not support it. Politicians and the mainstream media would be wise to heed these words.

Recently, a group financially backed by the 92-year-old George Soros has taken control of eighteen Spanish-language, conservative radio stations, forming innocently named Latino Media Network. This is the same individual that for several election cycles has been successfully backing progressive district attorneys and prosecutors in multiple key cities throughout the country with the stated aim of not prosecuting criminals, thus allowing many hardened criminals to roam the streets. The result, since 2020, is that most of these cities have tragically observed record increases in most types of crime, including homicide. Minorities, including Latinos, have been the main victims of such progressive strategies. It appears that the not so transparent goal for this new radio network is to convert the message and control Latino opinion by delivering a leftist agenda. Unfortunately, these voices are likely to run contrary to family, faith, and patriotism, the conservative values most Latinos hold dear to their heart.

It would seem to me that the network which rapidly embraces old-school, balanced, accurate journalism and not only one-sided, left-leaning opinion pretending to be "news" will capture the vast Latino audience, each with its unique nuances, in search of simple truth. What is the harm with an approach of treating the audience with respect by presenting both sides of the political discourse and letting people form their own opinion? Some may say it's about the ratings! Well, the fact is that in 2021-2022 the mainstream media has experienced the most drastic decline in ratings in decades. So, continuing with this same "free-fall" strategy seems suicidal (CNN Plus anyone?). Perhaps the old statement from John 8:32, "The truth will set you free," could be embraced by the mainstream media to reconnect with viewers and attract new listeners. The current challenge to Latinos is to seek truth in journalism by watching different sources with different agendas as well as searching for the myriad of independents. Then, and only then, can one at least have a more complete picture of each situation or story.

This is a tough task, as it truly requires a Sherlock Holmes detective ability to separate one-sided opinion versus actual news, and facts supported by solid evidence. Please do not take hate or racist-appearing stories promoted by the mainstream media as fact unless you have done extensive research to evaluate the veracity of the report. Sadly, almost for the first time in journalism history in the

U.S., the corporatist mainstream media as a whole has discredited itself into almost irrelevancy. I challenge Latinos at large (and truly, all who consume media) to please not allow yourselves to be manipulated like a child falling for the cheap tricks of a birthday party clown. This is about being diligent so that in the end we have more facts and not mere one-sided, manufactured bias being thrown our way as the absolute truth. Let's do our own research to get the actual details and facts from different sources for this is the optimal way to honestly try to understand everyone, including those that disagree with us, so that we may all agree to work together to continue to build a better country.

LATINOS, EDUCATION, AND ECONOMICS

On a cool, drizzly, early morning prior to heading to the medical office where a busy full day of patients would await me, I made a pit stop at my usual Starbucks in the affluent Knox Henderson area of Dallas. While I waited for my regular venti dark roast with steamed vanilla milk, stevia, and a bit of cinnamon I noticed the gathered well-dressed, restless crowd also waiting for their order, mostly Caucasian and one or two African Americans. This store had recently re-opened after several months of closure on account of the Covid-19 pandemic. Across the street a building had been demolished in late 2019 and since January of 2020 a brand-new, multilevel structure had been rapidly erected over ten months. I glanced to see the on-going work and noticed several dozen workers busy working on all the different floors, some even perilously balancing from narrow beams situated on the various levels of the project. What was not surprising to me, perhaps neither to anyone else waiting for their Starbucks coffee, was the racial make-up of the workers. All appeared to be brown-skinned Latinos, in contrast to the predominant white coffee aficionados inside the shop. This has been the norm in Texas for several decades, rather than the exception. These workers, from what I could tell, had continued their labor uninterrupted, virus or no virus. The same can be said for the remodel project of the Katy Trail, a path that conveniently traverses the city for walkers, runners, skaters, and bike riders that caters to upscale Dallas residents. During the pandemic the trail closed for safety reasons, yet the Latinos kept on working. As I drove that morning to the clinic along South Collins Road in Arlington, Texas, past the Dallas Cowboys Stadium (now called the AT&T Stadium) there was a multilane two- to three-mile-long road reconstruction and resurfacing project. Needless to say, you the reader, may have already guessed without hesitation as to the racial make-up of the workforce on that wet morning. I slowed down, opened my window, and asked some of the workers when the project would be completed. I immediately recognized the Mexican Spanish accent. For some of us accustomed to recognizing the different Spanish accents that distinguish the various Latino ethnicities, just as different as Anglo accents, Mexican Spanish is distinguishable, even from the different regions in Mexico. No doubt, from what I could see, most of the workers that morning were of Mexican descent and the only white I identified was a forty-something fellow comfortably sitting in his truck drinking a Starbucks coffee. I wonder if he was just a laborer on a coffee break or the boss. "Estaca Brown!" Is this surprising to anyone any more in the U.S.?

Many would offer that for most individuals the attainment of the "American Dream" within a Western Civilization model has been largely made possible by higher education and entrepreneurship. As a firm believer in higher education as the foundation needed to avoid personal and multigenerational dependency on welfare programs, and ultimately to build family household wealth, I have attempted to emphasize such values to my four children, who have all embraced university educations. However, this has been far from the norm for Mexican Americans and most other Latinos. According to the U.S. Census Bureau and the Pew Research Center, in 2016 the percent of 18-24-year-old Latinos enrolling in college was 43%, with about 52% of those attending a four-year university program and 48% two-year associate degree programs. As positive as these important trends may be, one can reasonably ask how many actually graduate. In 2019 only 18.8% of Latinos 25-29 years of age had earned a bachelor's degree or higher, while 40.1% of whites, 26.1% of Backs and 58.1% of Asians had attained such degrees. For comparison, foreign-born, first-generation Latinos, such as someone like me, possessed a university degree or higher only 9.8% of the time. The recent doubling of the number of mostly U.S.-born Latinos graduating with a four-year degree program or higher shows progress with still great room for further growth.

Aside from the historical low education level of their older relatives, for most young U.S.-born Latinos the difference in cost between community college versus a university education, public or private, plays a major factor in enrollment and graduation. At this time Latino students have about half the debt of other racial groups, indicating the significantly higher community college enrollment than whites and Blacks. As noted above, this all translates into Latinos still lagging behind the other racial groups in obtaining four-year university degrees. Does this mean that Latinos may well be confining themselves into an underclass status in the U.S., mostly as manual laborers? Or will they in time join in greater numbers the middle and upper socioeconomic classes? The answer to this question is complex. On the one hand, opportunities exist for willing Latino students to obtain a multitude of financial aid packages for both community colleges and universities. Many Latino high school students simply do not know how or where to apply for these scholarship and financial aid programs or how to navigate application and transfer processes.

In many instances the parents are the ones guiding the application effort and in the case of some Latinos, the parent(s) are not well versed on this often-complicated application process. I suspect this may also be the case for some Black and Native American students. Then there are the historic Latino cultural and family barriers that have gradually been overcome by the mostly U.S. born Latinos, especially when these young students become aware, as mentioned previously, that Latinos whose head of the family is a college graduate earn twice that of those who are not, and attain a family net worth four times higher. This is a gradual process that will probably take several generations. For Latinos with strong family ties in their country of origin, especially in the case of Mexican Americans, who frequently send financial aid back "home," it is inevitable that they compare themselves to those who stayed in Mexico. Many now own a home, some run or own a business, while others rely on steady employment, and most enjoy a close family whom they support with vast numbers living in nice secure neighborhoods. In other words, large sectors of the Mexican American and other Latino have greatly benefited from the advances made over the last sixty years and as a consequence have attained their own version of the "American Dream" or as I like to call it "Mexican Contentment."

Some may say this modest low-level version of the "Dream" would never suffice for most whites, especially those in the middle and upper classes. However, if one makes a priority list of what's truly important in life, Mexican Americans seem to have a fresh and optimistic take on this concept, one derived from authentic contentment that all those small, everyday, seemingly mundane experiences bestow upon us. When a survey was conducted asking Mexican men what was "most important to you in life," the top answers were to be a good father, to take care of family, to be a good husband, and to provide educational opportunities for their children. In addition, other surveys show a prioritization of access to quality and affordable healthcare and fair legal immigration laws. These priorities are certainly shared by many others in the world, but it is particularly inspiring that for many Mexican Americans with the privilege of living in the U.S., these are indeed their top priorities.

WHAT ABOUT THE RACISM?

For centuries, Mexican Americans have lived in what constitutes the U.S. and since 1848 most already in southwestern territories became U.S. citizens. Yet in facing the prolonged discrimination and racism of the early American period outlined in the previous chapters, Mexican Americans and other Latinos responded in predictable fashion. In his excellent 2018 published article titled "Mexican Americans: A Sociological Introduction," Phillip E. Lampe describes in detail the six possible ways victims of such prejudice respond. They are acceptance, assimilation, avoidance, accommodation, aggression, and organized protest.

According to Mr. Lampe, Mexican Americans that accepted racism were in fact accepting negative stereotypes and demeaning treatment and were likely to develop poor self-esteem and even self-hatred. In the encounter with the Anglo, the Mexican was made to feel even more alone. This was a point made by Octavio Paz in "The Labyrinth of Solitude." In this book-length essay, he wrote about the isolation already felt by Mexicans, who having inherited two cultures, the indigenous and the Spanish — and the Anglo more readily accepting the "whiter" Spanish part — was pushed into denying a part of this identity. The Mexican ended up forever stuck in a world of abject emotional inferiority and solitude, and unable to better himself, as he was likely to fail on account of prevalent racism.

Other Mexicans simply elected to adopt the concept of avoidance, preferring to live with his own people in cozy friendly "barrios," limiting social and church-related activities to segregated Mexican neighborhoods. This, of course, slowed assimilation and created a Mexican American culture that felt more like a version of their former home. For the many Mexicans who wished to assimilate to the predominant Anglo culture, it was simply not possible unless they were more "white" Spanish, well-educated, well-spoken in English, and preferably affluent. In some ways, these assimilated Mexicans were accepting that the Anglo culture was superior to his own, and hence he must do his best to shed his Mexican nature. Educated Mexicans south of the border gradually came to repudiate assimilated, largely uneducated Mexicans north of it, seeing them as ignorant traitors of their language and native culture even though many of these poor Mexican immigrants to the U.S. had been the target of racial and socioeconomic discrimination in Mexico.

Eventually most Mexicans and Latinos that accommodated to the Anglo culture did so by accepting racist stereotypes and opting not to react with aggression, but rather by learning to work and live as best as they could under the circumstances. For many it was a matter of exercising an acceptable balancing act of both cultures, often relying on the Catholic Church to provide guidance. This attitude has allowed many Mexicans and Latinos in general to carve out their version of the "American Dream," sometimes called, as I mentioned, "Mexican Contentment" with their place in American society. As far as aggression is concerned, I respectfully differ from Mr. Lampe. As a Mexican American the next response to racism on my list is assembly, the right to peacefully organize and protest. This has been the predominant pattern for Mexican Americans and Latinos as previously noted in the segment relating the leadership of César Chávez. It is my personal observation and bias that Mexican Americans and Latinos at large by far prefer to voice their complaints or list of grievances in a peaceful fashion, opting not to riot and destroy property, instead following the effective examples set by Dr. Martin Luther King, Jr. and César Chávez.

In 2020 when a Latino was killed by a police officer, there were several short-lived peaceful protests in various places in California and New Mexico, receiving minimal media coverage. None deteriorated into destructive rioting and looting. Much can be said, again my personal belief, for the fact that Latinos know too well the tremendous effort required in the construction of properties or operating a small family business, so that the concept of property destruction as a form of protest is almost completely foreign to them. When an atrocity occurs, such as the murder of Mexican Americans and Mexican citizens in El Paso by a deranged white supremacist, Mexicans do not choose to become the squeaky wheel that galvanize public opinion, societal outrage, and sustained widespread media coverage. Could one possibly say Mexican Americans have simply accommodated to the predominant Anglo culture, accepting their circumstances and generally do not make enough noise, so they are easily neglected on such issues? Perhaps this is in part why my children asked if Mexicans matter. They are pointing out that Mexican Americans are for the most part neglected by the media, the political establishment, and society at large, except on election years. Also, that Mexican Americans and all other Latinos are labeled as a single group, a pan-Latino monolith: the "Latino Vote." A grossly shortsighted and inaccurate vision largely underestimating even basic differences among the different Latinos. Why is this?

It appears that most Americans (Anglo, Hispanic, or other

heritage) do not know the history of Mexicans and other Latinos in the U.S. Perhaps by now the reader of this narrative has a better understanding of this history. The other implication that my kids are making is that if Latinos went on a destruction and rioting spree in a major U.S. city, an event I would never endorse or hope for, after the unfortunate death of a Latino at the hands of a police officer, then perhaps more media coverage and national attention would result. Once again, I do not believe, even for a second, that this would be the way to actually accomplish the desired goal of bringing attention to instances of allegations of police brutality affecting Mexican Americans and other Latinos.

A seat at the table of dialogue to take corrective action on this and other important social topics requires facts, civility, and a large dose of common sense. To that effect, I challenge the reader to step out of the usual media driven black-white binary, correct as it may be, and name ONE Latino of the more than 1000 killed over the last seven plus years during interactions with the police according to The Washington Post database. Really, can you name ONE?

> A seat at the table of dialogue to take corrective action on important social topics requires facts, civility, and a large dose of common sense.

A BRIEF PERSONAL NOTE ON EDUCATION

Beyond the above aspects, if one has the opportunity, the pursuit of education remains a personal choice driven by a desire to become more skilled, more academically educated, and better equipped to compete nationally and internationally at the highest levels now and in the future. I understand that not everyone is meant to achieve higher education, even when the opportunity presents itself. Those preferring to stop their educational path on graduation from high school, they must know the road ahead is an uncertain one. It is imperative that a concrete plan is carefully selected. Among the dozens of available options for many Latinos could be a shorter trade school programs that provide a definite marketable skill in a variety of fields that can provide immediate employment, a good income well above minimum wage, job security, and the possibility of starting one's own business. Taking an online or night school business or accounting class could add to that necessary knowledge to succeed in a competitive business environment, especially in elaborating a business plan and obtaining business loans. In essence, the "American Dream," or any individual's version of it, can be achieved via different pathways for Latinos.

HOUSEHOLD INCOME MATTERS

With the above college and university graduation percentages in mind, it would not be surprising to note that the 2019 average household income was $56,113 for Latinos, $45,438 for Blacks, $76,057 for whites and $98,174 for Asians. The long list of disparities that existed prior to the 1960s, especially in education and business opportunities, still matter today. Why are Asians the richest per capita individuals in the U.S.? The simple answer is that large numbers of Asian immigrants arriving in the U.S. have already attained a university degree in their nation of origin and once in the

U.S. most prioritize and sacrifice to ensure that their children obtain a college education. A similar cultural phenomenon is observed in the Indian American community, the second per capita most affluent people in the U.S.

Most would agree that higher education has been and continues to be the great economic equalizer in U.S. society. Middle and upper socioeconomic classes of all ethnicities seek higher education for their children at a similar rate. The issue is that fewer Latino and Black families are considered middle or upper socioeconomic class. According to the Brookings Institute, middle class is defined as prime age-adults (25 to 54 years of age head of household) between the 20th and 60th percent of national household income quintiles (income range $30,000 to $86,000 – depending on household size). In 2017, the middle class was comprised as follows: Hispanics about 22%, Blacks 14%, and whites 55%. These families are not considered rich, but are in a position, with some sacrifice, to help their children attain some form of higher education. Another metric that correlates with higher education status are household income levels in the top 40% (greater than $86,000). This elite group is made up by 13% of Hispanics, 8% of Blacks, and 67% of whites. When one analyses these socioeconomic status groups and the respective percentages of each ethnic group, then places them in parallel to the 2019 percent of Hispanics (18.8%), Black (26%), and white (40.1%) with a bachelor's degree or higher, it becomes evident that household income correlates with higher education attainment.

Given the income levels, one could actually say Hispanics are still lagging behind on obtaining college degrees and that Black students are taking more advantage of their opportunities. By this measure, whites are underperforming. In the next twenty-five years it is anticipated that the percent of middle-class minorities will increase such that whites will be about 49% of that group. This should result in more minorities graduating with college degrees.

Since the late 1960s, educational opportunities have been available to all individuals of all races who choose to obtain such degrees. The above income statistics are impressive indeed, yet obviously there is still much room for improvement in the Black and Latino communities. It is my belief that we are at a crucial crossroads in this country. Do we allow ourselves to become even more dependent on big government and increasing welfare programs, or do we become the architects of our own success on our own terms? Making the second choice means shedding all negative stereotypes and vestiges of any victimhood mentality that easily blames another — the white man — for our own mistakes or prior failures, instills in us paralyzing fear, weakens our resolve, and makes each one of us doubt our unique ability and potential.

HIGH SCHOOL

The pathway to improving one's economic status and increasing opportunities starts with high school graduation rates. The U.S. Public High School Graduation Rates for 2017-2018 published by NCES reported rates for Latinos of 81%, Blacks 79%, whites 89%, and Asians 92%. For Hispanics the high school graduation rate was 60% in 1990, clearly pointing to the dramatic increase in this vital accomplishment in a short time frame. The argument can be made that the influence of foreign-born parents and other relatives who are first generation immigrants lacking higher education historically played a role in lower graduation rates for Latinos. For many Latino families, the reality is that the extra income earned by their children has been a necessity for a family to just get by, often locking young Latinos into a lifelong pathway as unskilled or poorly skilled laborers. The good news is the trend of more assimilated Latino generations embracing the necessity of a high school diploma and a community college or university education as a more certain path for success in the U.S. There is, however, one concerning factor to overcome, since it can rapidly derail the above trends. The increasing minority single parent households and poverty rates afflicting Latino and Black communities at horrendously high rates are calamitous for the children in those homes. Reducing these rates should be the focus of national economic policies that incorporates child and adult education, community safety, adult skill acquisition, job training programs, avoiding teen pregnancy, and promoting successful marriages and the important role of the father in a child's life.

WHERE YOU LIVE MATTERS?

Where people live matters in the U.S. The living arrangements of children eighteen years of age and under significantly contribute to the racial differences in the above statistics. In 2013, 57% of Latino kids lived in a two-parent home while 32% lived in a single mother household. The poverty rate in this latter group was 52%. For Black children, 32% were living in a two-parent home, 58% in a single mother household with poverty rate of 55% for this latter situation.

For whites in 2013, the numbers were 73% of children living in a two-parent household, 18% in a single mother home with a poverty rate of 34% for this last group. Asian children lived with two parents 83% of the time, 11% with a single mother and a poverty rate of 24%. As we've seen with statistics previously covered, single-parent households are far more common in the Latino and Black communities, with extreme poverty rates more than 20% higher than whites and Asians. What's the unfortunate impact of all of this? Simply stated, a direct relationship is readily apparent between disproportionate poverty rates, high school drop-out rates, and lower enrollment and graduation rates in community colleges and universities. All of this results in lower household income and wealth, and ultimately more dependence on government-sponsored welfare programs.

The good news is that these trends have improved for Latinos and Blacks over the last decade, translating into higher high school and college graduation rates for Latinos. The argument can be made that the civil rights and welfare programs that started with LBJ's Great Society of the mid-1960s had a great impact in terms of eliminating institutional racism and providing wealth redistribution, but there are still large numbers left behind. Each time there is a depression of the economy, Blacks and Latinos suffer the most in terms of both unemployment and poverty rates, resulting in a "yoyo" effect on government dependence. Without a doubt, many minority individuals have taken advantage of educational programs, started businesses, then invested wisely, and avoided long-term government welfare dependence as they advanced professionally and economically largely unimpeded, while seamlessly thriving and fitting into the established and predominant U.S. social and economic model. Fortunately, this is the current trend in our society, but much work remains with the many who have remained in a status of generational welfare dependency.

ELEMENTARY EDUCATION

The remaining inequities can in large part be attributed to public elementary education in the U.S. The National Assessment Education Program (NAEP) reported that from 1975 to 2012, reading and mathematics proficiency showed significant performance differences between whites, Blacks, and Hispanics. In terms of reading proficiency, white nine-year-olds demonstrated scores twenty to thirty points higher than Black and Hispanic children. A similar pattern was found to persist in thirteen-year-olds. The same striation was shown in mathematics proficiency for students from age nine and persisting to age seventeen. Asian children outperformed all others, especially in calculus. Furthermore, Asians and whites were one and a half to two times more likely to take advanced placement credits in high school than Latino and Black students. These courses are more likely to prepare students for academic success in science, technology, engineering, and mathematics (STEM classes) at the university level. An educational policy maker may take these observations from the NAEP and conclude that public education is not providing sufficient proficiency to minority students prior to age nine.

This is certainly not an easy matter to resolve, but it is imperative

> Do we allow ourselves to become even more dependent on big government and increasing welfare programs, or do we become the architects of our own success on our own terms?

that every effort is made towards correcting these deficits through strategies that involve community leaders and organizers interested in improving the academic proficiency of these young students, as well as employing committed teachers that are paid appropriately, retired volunteers who may wish to participate, provision of educational tools and modern technology, regular parental school involvement, secure and clean schools, after-school academic, sports and arts programs, and private sector investments into each of these neighborhoods. I cannot understate the critical role of the parents (including fathers) and other caregivers such as grandparents, in being consistently invested in their children's education and every other aspect of their lives, but also in providing, as much as possible, a less stressful home and community environment that avoids the violence, abuse, and drug exposure that deprives children of school attendance, participation, academic achievement, and ultimate success in life. Undoubtedly, the lockdowns during the pandemic actually worsened the situation, as mentioned previously, with most minority children falling behind on academics and social development, a mistake that we cannot afford to repeat. We understand it is an extremely difficult task, requiring perhaps a holistic gradual solution, but it is a priority and a matter of national emergency, otherwise, the U.S. educational level will continue to lag behind most of the western world and Asian nations.

THE WELFARE STATE

Are Latinos now experiencing what I call "The Great Society Mexican Style"? Although poverty rates did initially decrease significantly for minorities from 1959 to 1969 as noted previously, unfortunately these welfare programs created a dependency on government. One could say that in time the clear outcome was "unintended" collateral damage detrimental to minorities. The effect on the African American household was a steady reward for single, poor, uneducated mothers to become "married" to big government, while poor married couples or couples living under the same roof raising children received less support. Unfortunately, this incentive created intergenerational dependency with an alarming increase in single, poor mothers living in decaying inner cities, struggling to raise their children. What was thought to be a tragic statistic in 1964, a single parent household rate of 25%, has more than tripled to the current 77%. This has resulted in a catastrophic set of circumstances, like a domino effect, of poorly educated children, teen pregnancy, poverty, crime, high incarceration rates, and substance abuse often a consequence of despair. Has this also occurred at least in some part in the Latino community? Let's first look at past and present statistics for beneficiaries of the most common welfare programs.

There are approximately seventy-nine welfare programs that support about 21% of the U.S. population. The main four are: Temporary Assistance for Needy Families (TANF), Food Stamps (SNAP), Medicaid, and Housing Assistance. Minorities have the highest rate of participation in the welfare system. However, it is a misperception to think whites do not receive significant help. In fact, 2019 statistics demonstrate that 43% of the federal welfare budget is received by whites, 28% by Hispanics, and 23% by Blacks. According to the U.S. Census Bureau, in 2015, 13.4% of whites were on one or more welfare programs, 27.6% of Blacks, and 35.5% of Latinos. The main risk factors contributing to these results are single motherhood, low education, unemployment, and poverty. Then there is the stigma that must be overcome to accept one or more welfare programs, especially from generation to generation. Once the stigma is overcome, in essence a negative for the individual and society, it is more likely that people will remain dependent for life and serve as a negative role model for their children to follow the same path of dependency. Interestingly, in 1994-1995, according to The National Academies of Sciences, Engineering and Medicine (NAP), 11.8% of Hispanics received TANF (formerly called AFDC), Blacks at 14.0%, and whites at 2.7%. For Medicaid the numbers were 24.5% for Hispanics, 27% for Blacks, and 8.3% for whites. SNAP (Food Stamps) were given to 20.1% of Hispanics, 23.3% of Blacks, and 5.7% of whites. Lastly, 9.1% of Hispanics were given housing assistance, 15.3% of Blacks, and 3.5% of whites. During the depression years of 2009-2012, on an average month, Hispanics received assistance at a rate of 36.4%, Blacks at 41.6%, and whites at 13.2%. With an improving economy from 2017 to 2019 (pre-COVID 19) and the lowest unemployment rates in history for Hispanics and African Americans, in 2018 the total welfare budget decreased by 5%. SNAP dependence decreased by some ten million families. Prosperity in the economy has a significant effect on welfare program utilization by all groups. Since 2010, Latinos have accounted for about 52% of the nearly ten million in population growth, resulting in many newcomers, including vast numbers of non-Mexicans, needing welfare support, even as many more established Latinos are coming off it.

Since early 2021, especially with the open-border crisis, more than two million undocumented immigrants have crossed the Mexico-U.S. border illegally. The vast majority are economic migrants and not genuine asylum seekers. Their provenance is mainly from the Central American triangle countries. Unfortunately, the reality is that aside from the treacherous journey mostly on foot, tragic deaths during the crossing of the Rio Grande, the dramatic increase in dangerous and lethal drug trafficking (fentanyl), there are also numerous human rights violations, including the rape of many vulnerable women. These atrocities, at times committed on Mexican territory, and others subjected by force to human trafficking operations once in the U.S., have caused a very real human cost and tremendous resentment mostly aimed at Mexicans. It has become evident that Mexican Americans and these newcomers do not get along on account of a variety of different educational and cultural characteristics that result in frequent violence. Mexican Americans have come to reject the intrusion of these migrants into their communities, thus altering their comfortable status quo. Also, they are opposed to the new migrants' intent on obtaining substantial "free" government welfare support. Recently, it has become evident that several not-for-profit organizations have established quasi-business services that are provided to the federal government in exchange for millions in funding that is then passed on to the new immigrants. Mexican Americans and other right-leaning groups are outraged by this sleight of hand.

Those that are allowed to remain in the U.S., with a court date scheduled at some future point, that hopefully they will keep, have had to be supported with some money, phones, and even expensive hotel stays. Others are bused or flown from the border to various destinations and then in many instances provided various means of support by the not-for-profit organizations. The ultimate cost to the taxpayers and to the economy at large is difficult to estimate. It is highly likely that these millions of newcomers will end up on multiple welfare programs that are already taxed to the maximum, resulting in an even more rapidly increasing yearly federal deficit and the current more than thirty trillion dollars of national debt. ($30,000,000,000,000!)

Several questions remain. Why have Latin Americans become more dependent on the various welfare programs since 1995? Is this increasing dependency a sign of an unhealthy socioeconomic future for many Latinos, especially Mexican Americans, with the creation of a larger and larger underclass? Have the policies that made welfare programs more available (like removing the renewal procedures based on continued need and replacing it with automatic renewals of benefits) promoted a dependency, with higher single parent households that may parallel the phenomenon seen in the decades after the launching of the "Great Society" of the mid-1960s? Can the U.S continue to afford an open-border immigration policy when currently there are some forty-six million people in the U.S. living in poverty not eligible for any welfare and approximately thirty million or more without any healthcare insurance coverage? As implied above, this policy has adversely impacted Mexican Americans living in the southwestern states and Texas. Mexican Americans are increasingly frustrated, and feel completely neglected by federal authorities since the perception is that the illegal immigrants get all the benefits. In fact, Texas' 34th Congressional District, which was held for more than a hundred years by one party, recently flipped to the opposing party, clearly reflecting this sentiment. It is likely that this same phenomenon will occur in the upcoming election cycles. In addition, this year there have been record-breaking numbers of deaths near the U.S. border. The International Organization for Migration's Missing Migrants reported 728 missing or deceased migrants in 2021 and so far, 290 in 2022, most of them on U.S. soil. Many Mexican Americans living along the southern border have directly experienced this appalling situation, which some characterize as an invasion, are upset that the federal government appears to continue to ignore the crisis and pay lip service to strategies that may help curve the situation.

ROLE MODELS

According to the Hamilton Project Report by the Brookings Institute, in 2016 a pre-tax household income for a family of 4 below $24,229 constituted poverty. This is what it means to be poor in America. In 1980 there were 29.3 million people living in poverty and in 2014 the number had increased to 46.7 million. Welfare programs can marginally elevate many on the threshold of the above income level, at least conceptually, yet the reality is that they remain poor and insufficiently educated. In spite of educational progress, a Latino underclass appears to be growing in the U.S., especially if one includes the more recent and current massive legal and mostly illegal migrations from Central America and southern Mexico. What needs to be done?

There are no shortcuts to resolve these serious matters. A bright trend has been emerging for Latinos, especially for the two-thirds born in the U.S., who have dropped out of high school at the lowest rates ever (~10%) and been able to obtain higher education degrees at increasing numbers. From the prior discussion, it is evident that greater emphasis on providing high quality education from kindergarten through high school, with consistent parental involvement, to prevent kids from falling behind academically, and then solid policies that provide equal opportunities for high performing students to pursue college pathways are important. For those not wishing that journey, job training opportunities should be instituted promptly. These changes would result in reducing poverty and, in less than a generation, increase individual and community prosperity.

There are already millions of highly educated Latinos succeeding in the U.S. economy, competing for the highest positions and also able to provide worthy role models for younger generations. The fact is that mainstream media and social media platforms have historically neglected Latino culture and successes, while for the most part promoting negative stereotypes, criminality, and illegal immigration, does not help the Latino community in any way. Hollywood has contributed to this neglect, as noted previously, with Hispanics accounting for only 4.5% of all speaking parts in the 1200 most popular movies from 2007 to 2018 and only 3% of roles as protagonists. Latinos are about 18% of the U.S. population and purchase 23% of movie tickets. When a Latino does have a role in a production, with few exceptions, it is usually one of a maid, nanny, cook, landscaper, grape picker, janitor, waiter, dishwasher, construction worker, mechanic, driver, pool boy, petty criminal, western bad guy, drug dealer coyote, drunk with a large mustache, drunk without a mustache, rapist, unbathed, unemployed loser, and a myriad other classic well-ingrained stereotypes that even extend to cartoon characters. Some movies even promote Latinos, especially Mexicans, speaking in thick, unsavory accents that are intended to ridicule their apparent lack of education and alleged cultural ignorance. What would be the response from the African American community and woke mainstream media if these inequities continued to occur to their talented artists?

Needless to say, all of these so-called liberal institutions, apparently pro-minority, pro-gender, pro-LGBTQ+, and all for equality, have in no uncertain hypocritical terms failed the Latino community en masse. These institutions have also in many aspects betrayed Latinos by indoctrinating young, impressionable Anglo movie goers with pervasive derogatory images. Then there's the usual cheap joke full of wink-wink innuendo often told by a white man to another white man that, "Those Mexican soap-operas are so hot, especially with the volume off." No need for Latinos to continue to embrace these supposed elite individuals pretending to be role models, including the news media biased, opinion peddlers, Hollywood personalities, and millionaire athletes, who have little real knowledge of humble grassroots Latino communities and poor people. They seek to influence the populace to think in monolithic terms to serve a purpose best suited to their political ideologies and in so doing deprive or highjack people's ability to think for themselves and develop their own unique ideas. It is shameful that so many minority celebrities today partake in the sale of fast foods and soft drinks, among other harmful products to one's health, all with the intent of influencing unsuspecting minorities. It is indeed best to focus on one's parents as genuine role models, or the great, inspirational teachers that are paid an infinitesimal amount compared to the above celebrities, and perhaps the many wonderful local professionals and community and church leaders.

Latinos today find themselves at a crossroads. The first choice is one of reliance on government welfare programs resulting in an expanding underclass, forever subservient to and followers of the elite upper classes. The second one consists of embracing the more difficult path that requires seizing educational opportunities and in short time catapulting millions of Latinos to compete at the highest level of a free market economy. The latter choice infers attaining far more political involvement at all levels, including the federal government in Washington, D.C. The fact is, that compared to African Americans, Mexican Americans have been and continue to be underrepresented in federal political circles, especially when one considers the forty million or so individuals of Mexican descent in the U.S. In contrast, Cuban Americans, a group that counts less than 2 million in the U.S., have far more representation in Washington government positions. Over the last fifty years, this phenomenon has not been due to any racist intent or discriminatory policies, but to simple under-preparation in the educational arena by significant numbers and under-participation by qualified meritorious Mexican Americans who should be throwing their lot into national politics. This is a challenge for Mexican Americans moving forward to attain a bigger voice in Washington, D.C.

LATINOS, VOTING AND POLITICS

Why do Mexican Americans have a history of not voting in elections? As it turns out, this is both a simple and difficult question to answer. I shall attempt to elucidate. Let's start with the concept that Latinos mainly identify by nation of origin. The concept of a "Pan-Ethnic-Latino" voice is a myth and one that politicians have not grasped for decades. Possible exceptions are the politically active and vocal Puerto Rican community in New York and the Cuban Americans in Florida. The rest of us are simply thrown into one massive amorphous category whose history, customs, culture, language differences, and nation of provenance simply do not matter. Simply stated, there is no Pan-Latino vote. This is an important issue since currently about 63% of the sixty million plus Latinos in the U.S.

are of Mexican decent. Additionally, the rest is made up of some five million Puerto Ricans, two million Cubans, just under 2 million from El Salvador, one and a half million Dominicans, some seven to eight million from various South American nations, and others the final million. Each of these groups holds tightly to its own country of origin's history, language, and culture, making for an underappreciated, diverse Latino presence in the U.S. This is critical for short-sighted political parties to comprehend in view of the rapidly growing population of present and future Latino voters, who no doubt will become more involved since about two-thirds or more

> Each group of Latinos holds tightly to its own country of origin's history, language, and culture, making for an underappreciated, diverse Latino presence in the U.S.

are now born in the U.S.

There are many Latino organizations in the U.S. whose mission has been to increase Latino civic and political participation. These include LULAC, MALDEF, National Council of La Raza, NALEO (National Association of Latino Elected Officials), Congressional Hispanic Caucus, and TRPI (Tomas Rivera Policy Institute). A separate, more regional group has been CANF (Cuban American National Foundation), mostly promoting Cuban American causes and political involvement. In spite of all these great organizations, Latino participation in voting, especially that of Mexican Americans, has historically been extremely poor. The passing of the Voting Rights Act (VRA) of 1975 was the first time the U.S. Congress recognized that four minorities had been excluded from voting, mostly on linguistic differences. These included Indian Americans, Alaskans, Asians, and Latinos. The VRA came as a result of the advancements mentioned earlier in the immigration laws of the 1960s that helped Blacks obtain fair voting access and removed the long-standing preferential policies for European immigrants while reducing discrimination against Latin American migration. In addition, politicians acknowledged the rapidly changing Latino diversity that would ensue beyond Mexican Americans, Cubans, and Puerto Ricans. The key strategies that VRA would promote via community activists were to increase naturalization rates, increase voter interest by addressing Latino issues such as education, immigration, healthcare, and public social programs, then register more Latino adults to vote. It was hoped that in time this would increase Latino political influence by electing more local and state officials, with some eventually reaching federal political offices.

In the end, these strategies aimed to move past the legacy of previous institutional exclusion and the voting lethargy or passivity that had traditionally infected Latinos, mostly Mexican Americans. It is a sad tale to examine the number of Mexican Americans that have made it to the federal government. No senators and only one Republican to the House of Representatives in the 1800s. Romulado Pacheco from California served from March 4, 1877 to February 7, 1878, when he lost an election contestation. He won a second term and served from March 4, 1879 to March 4, 1883, after which he retired. That's it! The post reconstruction exclusion from electoral politics applied to African Americans also targeted Mexican Americans. "Estaca Brown," as my uncle would say!

Manipulation of Mexican Americans by political machines controlled by white elites has operated by selecting hand-picked Mexican Americans to serve their purpose by encouraging the lesser-informed Mexicans to vote for their candidate. These repeated strategies over time led to a general depressing passivity and feeling of political impotence that has persisted until recently. Furthermore, compared to Black populations, the necessary civic infrastructure to promote political involvement did not develop at adequate rates among Mexican American communities, especially those located in rural areas. In addition, many of these Mexican Americans felt very real language and cultural exclusion from politics, an absent cohesive voice in Congress, and a lack of regional and national unity on issues important to their cause. In the period from 1900 to 2020 the number of Mexican Americans elected to the U.S. Senate has increased, with one Republican and five Democrats. Would that qualify as a gross underrepresentation over a 120-year time frame? How about the House of Representatives? The number here is much better with seven Republicans and fifty-three Democrats in the same timeframe.

Since the passing of the VRA in 1975, there has been a gradual increase in Latino political and voting participation. New immigrants, especially those from Central America and the Caribbean not in touch with U.S. culture and politics, take longer to assimilate and participate in the electoral process as compared to second and third or higher generation eligible adult voters. In the 1800 election the percent of the vote cast by Latinos was 2.6% out of a total of 93,066 total votes. By 2012 the Latino vote was 7.4% out of 118,583 total votes. That's only 8775 votes for a population of about 52,000 million

Latinos in the U.S. in 2012. Maybe these numbers help explain the historic overall Anglo neglect and possible lack of knowledge and only passing shallow interest about the various Latino communities and their particular issues. It appears that for 2020, the Latino vote was slightly over sixteen million, or about 10% of the overall vote, but it is not indicative that politicians truly "understand" each Latino community. Those states and counties with large Latinos voting, such as the southwestern states, and specifically Texas and Florida, given the current 2022 issues important to them, will definitely see a greater impact on state and presidential election results in the next few years.

Political issues most important for Mexican Americans are immigration policies that are fair-minded, consideration for possible amnesty programs, civil rights protections, publicly funded social services, cultural sensitivity, high academic quality to advance to university education, public safety, public transportation, and eliminating pockets of residual discrimination and racism wherever they may lurk. At this moment, gas prices and inflation of basic products, including groceries, occupy the kitchen table conversations for most Mexican Americans. Afterall, it is the minorities that are most affected by these issues.

In 2020, with the COVID-19 pandemic affecting the entire world and causing massive economic shutdowns, Mexicans and other Latinos, especially Latinas, experienced tremendous hardship, with an increase in unemployment higher than any other racial group. The country-wide imposed lockdowns on service-oriented sectors of the economy such as hotels, restaurants, office buildings where they work as custodians and domestic services, all accounted for the majority of layoffs. Mexican Americans and other Latinos still fear more lockdowns, higher unemployment, and higher taxes that may affect their burgeoning middle-class status. For many of these Mexican Americans, steady, uninterrupted employment is critical to their version of the "American Dream," since they are often found at the lower end of the middle class and provide for dependent family members living in Mexico. For Cuban Americans the talk of foreign policy and socialism so commonplace in the current national dialogue are both critical issues. Socialism is not an ideology that Cubans are willing to accept based on their personal, catastrophic, historical experience. Many other Latinos, such as Venezuelan Americans, with their recent upheaval, also feel the same repudiation towards socialist governments.

Sadly, however, Latinos still lag behind in actual voting numbers. Less than 50% of registered voters actually vote, which is 10% lower than Blacks and 20% lower than whites. Factors that contribute to lower voting participation include lower socioeconomic status, lower education level, and younger age. Interestingly, Latinos who are educated beyond high school and enjoy a higher socioeconomic status vote at the same rate as other educated white, Black, and Asian individuals. More than 30% of Latinos eligible to vote do not have a high school diploma compared to 12% of whites, contributing to lower Latino voting numbers. Latinos aged 18-24 only vote at a 25% rate, while those 25-44 years old do so 43% of the time and those older than 45 years of age vote at rates of 55-61%. Clearly there is much room for improvement in educating and promoting voter participation in the coming years, especially for the rapidly growing numbers of young Latinos. It is likely that the current economic situation and the crisis at the border, among other concerns, will galvanize more Latinos, and in particular Mexican Americans, to vote in the upcoming elections.

POLITICAL IDEOLOGY AND LATINOS

With the exception of Cuban Americans, other Latinos have historically voted for democratic candidates. Mexican American democratic partisanship is 49%, Republican 25%, and 36% consider themselves moderates. Puerto Ricans are 57% Democrat partisans, 19% Republican, and 21% moderate. Central and South Americans have 57% Democratic Party partisanship, 18% Republican, and 34% moderate. As stated earlier, Cubans are 41% Republican, 37% Democrat, and 28% moderate. Independents vary from 10-12% across all the above groups. One must reasonably ask why most Latinos, including Mexican Americans, prefer the democratic party or a more moderate position. This could be because Latinos in the U.S. have demonstrated more trust in government than non-Latinos, especially in larger government as

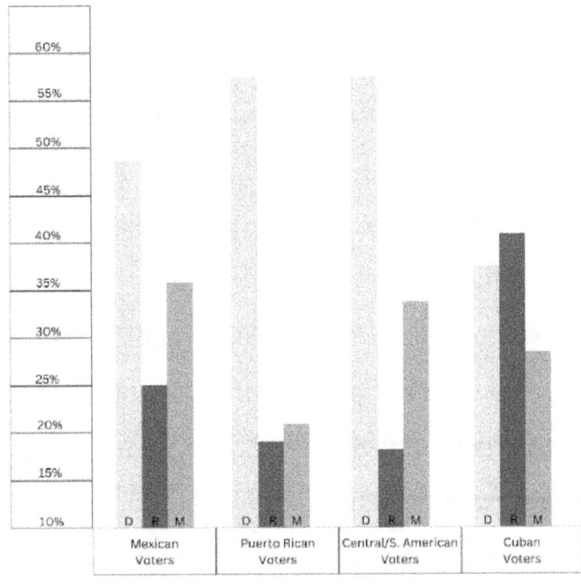

long as it funds social programs that cover education, welfare, and promote fair treatment of immigrants. A question that every Latino must consider is: Is the "American Dream" as promised by the architects of the "Great Society" out of reach for most of us, and instead are we blindly being herded towards a slaughterhouse I call "The American Underclass"?

In contrast to the promises of larger government and higher taxes, conservative talking points such as abortion, family values, the death penalty, and gender issues are of low priority to most Latinos at election time. Lower taxes and inflation resonate with most Latinos, but anti-immigrant rhetoric definitely does not. One other major issue Latinos heartily oppose is the much-discussed 2020 topic of defunding the police as was mentioned previously. Most in the Latino community prefer sensitivity retraining for individual officers and departments not performing up to standard on these important race issues. This includes the issue of police profiling and the fact that, according to the U.S. Bureau of Justice, the male prison population in 2018 was made up of 34% Blacks, 29% whites, and 24% Hispanics. This translates to an average incarceration rate of 5.8 times greater for Blacks and about 1.8 times greater for Hispanics than whites.

Interestingly, the Northeast has the highest incarceration rates for Hispanics, including Connecticut (6.6 Hispanics for every white), Massachusetts, Pennsylvania, and New York. It seems paradoxical that these traditionally more liberal, apparently pro-minority states with significant representation in federal politics should continue to incarcerate far more Latinos than the percent of the population would indicate. Is it that Latino "criminals" preferentially move to these states? The more likely explanation is that residents of these northeastern states, except for the Puerto Ricans, have not had as long a relationship with Mexican and Central American Latinos as the southern states and California. The incarceration policies enacted in the mid- to late-1990s have played a detrimental role in the lives of many of these newcomers seeking work and to improve the condition of family members back in their home country.

Such societal biases remain in specific areas and are the ones that police retraining must quickly address, especially for minor offenses. In the 2020 election, the economy, socialism versus capitalism, immigration policies, defunding the police, and healthcare were top priorities for Latinos at large. Moving forward, Latinos want to work, provide for their families, take advantage of educational and training opportunities, and not be told they are oppressed victims who must depend on government handouts. Nothing could be more repulsive to the Latino mindset. Furthermore, police retraining whenever and wherever is needed, not police defunding, is the common-sense approach since this will likely keep all communities safer, especially minority neighborhoods. With the dramatic increase in crime across the country in 2021-2022, and in particular large urban centers which have experienced a greater than 30% increase in the homicide rate, funding and retraining the police wherever necessary is the wish of most Latinos. Latinos see the police as a protector of the individual and community, not as a dangerous, intrusive enemy with a badge, to be avoided as a racist pariah. Addressing each of the above items for the current and future administrations will be challenging but essential to promote a long-lasting and nurturing relationship with most of the different Latinos.

LATINOS AND GDP

The myth that Latinos are poor and do not contribute to the U.S. economy is clearly false. The reality, according to the Latino GDP report

> 20% of construction companies in the U.S. are Latino-owned.

of 2017, is that Latinos in the U.S. had a GDP of $2.13 trillion, which would be the seventh largest in the world. Latinos definitely are not a drain on the U.S. economy. This GDP was greater than multiple nations including Canada, Italy, Brazil, and India. Once again, the reality is that the compounded annual growth rate (CAGR) for the Latino population in the U.S. is 2.9%, the third fastest in the world behind China and India. Without the Latino GDP the U.S. would lag behind China. The estimate in 2020 was that Latinos contributed to one-quarter of the U.S. GDP growth. From 2010 to 2015, the Latino work force grew by 2.5 million, while the non-Latino work force shrank by four thousand jobs. In 2019, The Joint Economic Committee reported that Latinos represented $2.3 trillion in economic activity, with U.S. Latino GDP growing 70% faster than non-Latinos. In addition, Latinos accounted for 70% of the increase of the U.S. workforce. Undocumented Latinos are often accused of being a drain on the U.S. economy, yet the reality is that they are an essential contributing part, especially in agriculture, thereby keeping food prices lower and lessening the need for imports. These same individuals also fill needed construction jobs that keep commercial, residential, and infrastructure projects moving forward, even during a pandemic. Interestingly, some 20% of construction companies in the U.S. are Latino-owned. Given the possible amnesty program promised by the current administration, it is likely that more Latinos will take advantage and legitimize even further their essential status in the U.S economy, as the rapidly growing backbone of the labor force across multiple sectors. I would not like to imagine the dramatic consequences upon the U.S. economy if by some stroke of bad luck Latinos, especially Mexicans, suddenly disappeared from the labor landscape for a few weeks, or even a day!

The above economic statistics are indicative of the significant contributions Latinos make to the U.S. economy. Currently the Latino population is 18.5% of the U.S. population (~64 million), with two-thirds born in the U.S., speaking English fluently, and 13% foreign-born who have become citizens. About 90% live in metropolitan areas and, according to the Brookings Institute, Latinos now make up 22% of the U.S. middle class. As more Latinos gain higher education in the coming decades, U.S. prosperity will come to depend not only on Latino manual workers, but on growing numbers of young professionals occupying higher positions in white collar institutions and on Latino-driven entrepreneurship. In addition, the U.S. armed forces have now come to depend on Latinos to defend the American way of life, with an impressive 25.7% of Marines and 22.2% of Army front-line servicemen having Hispanic ancestry.

The key issue here is for Latinos to earn a different position in society, including the private sector and highest political offices, based on hard work, dedication, education, ability, and merit, not on skin color, race, and ethnicity. We Latinos cannot and should not accept government or any other positions that we have not trully earned just to satisfy someone's manufactured minority-based or victim-based quota system. This is not true diversity. The diversity we Latinos are willing to accept is one independent of race, ethnicity, gender, and skin color, and instead one that defines diversity as bringing to the table individuals with different ideas, civilly dialoguing to understand different viewpoints so that we may reach logical and reasonable accords designed to improve society at large.

A NOTE ON 2020

As conflicts and tensions, national and international, continue to escalate, the U.S. careens towards the mid-term elections. Undoubtedly, the Russian invasion of Ukraine in February of 2022 and the rising temperature in U.S.-China relations, as well as the all-time record inflation in the U.S., significantly higher energy costs and criminality, have caused everyday Americans uncertainty about what comes next. How is an individual interested in working, providing for the family, respecting the rule of law, paying taxes, following their faith peacefully, and connecting with friends and community supposed to react and move forward productively without anxiety, a feeling of helplessness, and even some degree of despair? This current landscape is not one for creating peace of mind in most of us, especially as the political in-fighting continues to escalate. For most Latinos, the only way forward is to continue working, think carefully about the various issues of importance to their families and communities, not sit idly, as large numbers have done in the past, and instead go cast a vote in November. The Latino communities throughout the country must exercise, no matter which party or political leaders they support, their constitutional right at the ballot box. In essence, this is the way to change the landscape. For Mexican Americans, 2022 represents an awakening. With the monthly reported record numbers on illegal immigration, coming for the most part through a porous southern border, the message to the federal government, mostly from the most affected southern states, has been crystal clear: Stop the continuous massive flow of these largely economic migrants, and immediately enact a fair and robust legal immigration system.

Most Mexican Americans, even those of us whose families have been in the southern territories of the U.S. for some 400 years, fully recognize that the only true non-immigrants are the native indigenous populations, whose ancestors in many instances have been in the continental U.S. more than 10,000 years. The rest of us clearly usurped and encroached on these great lands. With an open border situation, the ones who are and will continue to be most affected are the minorities, especially the largest one of them all, the Mexican Americans. It is likely that these new migrants will end up residing in mostly Mexican neighborhoods, competing for similar jobs, with their children enrolled at the already saturated and academically underperforming local public schools, and elevate fear of increasing crime, drugs, and human trafficking. It is highly unlikely that predominantly middle, upper class, and elite areas throughout the country will be directly and visibly affected. Gimmicks to bus or fly migrants from the border states to Washington DC, New York, or other northeast cities should not be necessary to prove the point.

These mudslinging, childish tactics by both parties, hypocritical or not, mostly for political currency, do not convey a sense of seriousness and readiness to address the issues and finally fix them. I repeat what I've said before. What we need is a more robust, easier to navigate legal immigration system and protection from massive onslaughts of illegal immigrants.

LATINOS AND HEALTHCARE

COVID-19

Now, as a doctor, healthcare is a huge issue. Not just because

I'm a doctor, though, but because health impacts so many areas of life. Health is both effected by financial status and influences financial status. That's why this chapter tackles health as an issue equally important as the others discussed already, such as education, political involvement, and media-produced perceptions.

The most recent major issue impacting health, specifically that of minorities, has been the Covid-19 pandemic. Information has emerged from American Red Cross and the CDC that blood samples from donors in nine states, collected in mid- to late-December 2019, tested positive for Covid-19. This finding contradicts the previous report that the first case in the U.S. occurred on January 17, 2020. The percentage of blood samples that tested positive was very low, indicating that it was not yet widespread. Interestingly, only 3% of the donors had traveled outside of the U.S. in the prior 28 days and only 5% of those had traveled to Asia. Although cross reactivity with other coronaviruses may explain some of these findings, this report may indicate that the virus had already arrived in the U.S. by late November or early December 2019. To this we must consider that similar reports from Europe and South America indicate positive blood samples with the SARS-Cov-2 antibodies as early as July 2019. The first states affected were California, Oregon, and Washington. Then, in later December 2019, the spread included Connecticut, Iowa, Michigan, Wisconsin, Rhode Island, and Massachusetts. Could it be that the contagion moved from the west coast to the east coast? Is it possible there were early symptomatic cases in the U.S. in 2019 not recognized? In Italy there is now evidence that this novel coronavirus was spreading as early as September 2019.

Other countries, including Brazil, have reported positive blood samples from mid-summer 2019. This information may change the current narrative that the virus came from Wuhan, China, probably as a result of accidental exposure at the Wuhan Virology Institute. It would appear that at this moment we simply do not know where it came from. We cannot just assume it escaped from China months early. Or is it possible that poorly followed safety protocols at the Wuhan Virology Institute accidentally allowed the virus to gradually escape much earlier than previously suspected? We simply do not know for certain. What we can say is that the history of the pandemic will need to be re-written. For the purposes of this book, however, the question is: How does this impact Latinos?

SYNDEMIC

The unfortunate fact is that COVID-19 ravaged the Latino population in the U.S. According to CDC November 30, 2020, updated statistics (pre-vaccine), the Latino hospitalization and mortality rates were 4.1 and 2.8 times that of whites, respectively. For African Americans these rates were similar at 3.7 and 2.8 times that of whites. Native Americans and Alaska Natives had rates of 4.0 and 2.6 times that of whites. Also 45% of those twenty-one years of age and under dying from Covid-19 in 2020 were Latinos. These are clear indicators of the vastly increased risk of the above minorities.

As of February 15, 2022, the CDC reported Covid-19 cases and mortality data by race and ethnicity. Hispanics represented the highest share of cases relative to their share of the total population (24% vs. 18%). In terms of deaths, Hispanics had a more proportionate share of their total in the population (17% vs. 18%). African Americans experienced 13% of the cases and 14% of the deaths, both proportionate to their share of the total population (13%). Whites accounted for 54% of cases and 63% of deaths, in close proportion to their share of the population (60%). However, when data are adjusted to account for age, there are significant disparities for Hispanics and Blacks. Hispanics and American Indian or Alaskan Native had 1.5 times the number of cases of whites and Blacks. Compared to whites, deaths were 1.7 times higher for Blacks, 1.9 times for Hispanics, and 2.2 times higher for American Indians or

Alaskan Natives. Why are the death rates higher for the minorities?

Some have attributed these disparities to minorities having less access to healthcare, especially in states that did not expand Medicaid as part of the ACA. In addition, this susceptibility to Covid-19 is explained by the fact that Latinos and other minorities per capita have a higher incidence of comorbidities such as obesity, pre-diabetes, diabetes, and hypertension. There is definitely a genetic predisposition for Latinos, as well as American Indians, to develop metabolic syndrome early in adulthood. This consists of a cluster of chronic conditions associated with diabetes that place these minorities at higher risk of hospitalization and death from Covid-19 infection and long-haul Covid symptoms. Recently, it has become evident that Covid-19 can attack the insulin producing cells in the pancreas and, together with the acute inflammatory milieu, cause insulin resistance, and suddenly thrust a vulnerable individual into a pre-diabetic or full diabetic state, impairing the patient's immune response. This phenomenon could explain the increased hospitalization and mortality rates observed especially in Latinos and Native American populations. I experienced this phenomenon in November of 2020, working as a front-line physician, when I contracted Covid-19, becoming a pre-diabetic in just a few weeks in spite of losing some five pounds. It would be logical to conclude that the obesity-diabetic epidemic more prevalent among minorities in the U.S. collided with the Covid-19 pandemic, resulting in a syndemic, a term that refers to the synergistic interaction of these two, resulting in more severe health outcomes.

Different cultural behaviors can also contribute to higher risk of catching Covid-19, including frequent large family gatherings, living and working in concentrated places, and, at least initially, not being aware about the risk of infection. For example, large numbers of Mexican American adults (~19.3% as opposed to about 17.8% of all Latinos according to the 2017 Census Bureau statistics) have remained uninsured, especially those 18-39 years of age (~30%), and prior to the pandemic may not have seen a doctor in years. Hence, many were probably not aware of various ailments that they may have suffered from, some of these known to predispose to severe Covid-19 infection, including death. Latinos have traditionally been dedicated to working and supporting their families no matter the environmental and work conditions, which in many instances may have contributed to the risk of spreading the virus and exposure to a large inoculum, another factor that appears to have caused more severe disease and mortality in susceptible individuals. Latinos have a 50% lifetime risk of developing diabetes, with Mexican Americans, some Central Americans, and Puerto Ricans at the highest risk, and, as noted above, many severely affected by Covid-19 may not have initially been aware of their existing level of risk. In addition, is there a further genetic predisposing factor in some Latino groups, who possess more indigenous genetics and less European ancestry? After all, most indigenous Latinos and American Indians share similar ancestry dating back to the peoples that trace their origin to Native North Siberian and Southeast Asian (Mongolia and Manchuria) populations that crossed Beringia after the last glacier maximum melted some sixteen to eighteen thousand years ago, and rapidly populated the Americas. Could this explain in some fashion our shared predisposition to diabetes?

This novel coronavirus is known to attach itself to ACE2 receptors present throughout the body, including the lungs, cardiovascular, and gastrointestinal systems, including the pancreatic beta cells. These are the cells that produce the hormone insulin which facilitates the entry of glucose (sugar) into the cells. It appears Covid-19 can induce prediabetes in those not known to have this condition and push pre-diabetics to full diabetes by damaging the pancreatic beta cells. In addition, the cytokine storm brought on by Covid-19 results in inflammation throughout the body, including interfering with the binding of insulin to its receptor. This tragic metabolic situation results in impairment of the individual's immune system, not only further impairing the ability to quickly recover but also augmenting the risk of mores serious disease and death.

Is it possible that these mechanisms affect Latinos at a higher rate than whites? Other minorities such as Native Americans and some African American populations may also be at risk of the same phenomenon, partly explaining the observed higher mortality. A simple study to prove this would be to take tissue samples from the pancreas in different populations to assess the number of ACE2 receptors present and to perform insulin resistance studies in those currently infected with Covid-19 and those who have recovered. Regardless of the underlying reasons, the fact is that Latinos have been dramatically affected by the pandemic with disproportionate hospitalization and mortality compared to whites.

The reality is that coronavirus mRNA vaccines have shown effectiveness against severe disease requiring hospitalization and death, but not as previously thought in terms of preventing mild to moderate infection. The present administration, since January 2021, has successfully promoted widespread vaccination and boosters, especially to moderate and high-risk groups. According to the CDC, the latest data on adult Covid-19 vaccination, as of July 11, 2022, across the thirty-six states for which a vaccination rate could be calculated by race and ethnicity, demonstrated that 67% of Hispanics, 59% of Blacks and 64% of whites had received at last one dose of the vaccine. In fact, Hispanics had a higher vaccination rate than whites in twenty-two states. Interestingly, CDC statistics demonstrate that Hispanic children five to eleven years of age, as of July 11, 2022, had lower vaccination rates in most states than whites, and about the same as Blacks. In terms of boosters, Hispanics lag behind whites and Blacks by about 5-20% in most states. These statistics demonstrate that Hispanic adults generally embraced the CDC guidelines on Covid-19 vaccination recommendations. But what about their attentiveness to health overall?

IS THE CURRENT HEALTHCARE MODEL WORKING?

In the U.S. Latinos face three main challenges with respect to healthcare.

(1) Access to effective healthcare.

(2) Food Industry and diet.

(3) Understanding the need for preventive medical care and chronic disease management.

Instead of focusing on each of the above independently, I shall take the reader on a narrative that interweaves the above challenges through a description of the current status of Latinos and the U.S.

healthcare system. Keep these in mind as you read on. I'll start with the Hispanic Paradox. In addition, as an addendum for those who may have an interest, I will propose a possible better model for healthcare delivery in the U.S., especially important for minorities.

LONGEVITY AND PUBLIC HEALTH

Life expectancy in the U.S. has increased from forty-seven years at the start of the 1900s to a remarkable longevity for all ethnicities. Many would point to the nearly worldwide recent 200-year scientific journey with markedly improved prosperity, dramatic reduction in abject poverty, and technological and medical advances as the driving forces of our collective improved longevity. As my grandmother in Mexico would often say to me, while smirking, whenever I would inquire what the bloody Mexican Revolution of 1910 brought to the Mexican people, "The toilet and the light bulb, my little grandson!" For millions who grew up during times of hardship, including the Spanish Influenza Pandemic in 1918, Great Depression of the 1930s, two world wars fighting fascism and nazism, the North Korean War, Vietnam, and the recent 20-year war in the Middle East, there is a deep-felt appreciation and gratitude for all the "good" Western Civilization has bestowed upon us. This includes the toilet, the light bulb, other fantastic medical and scientific technologies, and perhaps for many, and most importantly, Judeo-Christian values, all contributing to our present society and longevity.

Currently, Asian Americans live longest with an average of 86.3 years, Latinos 81.9 years, whites 78.6 years, Native Americans 77.4 years, and African Americans 75.0 years. These differences are unexpected when it comes to Latinos. It's been called the Hispanic Paradox. The numbers don't make sense, especially when multiple factors point to the adverse healthcare circumstances Latinos regularly face. To begin, the Census Bureau statistics for 2017 show that about 17.8% of Latinos nationally were uninsured compared to 5.7% of non-Latino white individuals. These numbers do not take into consideration the number of undocumented immigrants that regularly need vital healthcare services but do not get them. Among Latinos the highest uninsured individuals were Central Americans at 27.2% and the Mexican Americans at 19.3%. In 2017, some 17.3 million Latinos were covered under Medicaid and another 4.8 million by Medicare, adding up to about 38.2% of Latinos dependent on public health insurance. This is a key political issue with Latinos, fearful that Medicaid and Medicare programs will dry up or suddenly be taken away by federal politicians.

To this effect, there are two basic questions. The first is why so many Latinos have come to depend on such entitlement programs. The second asks if these public programs, when applied to Latinos, actually succeed in preventing disease, educating patients about illness, lifestyle, and medicine, treating acute diseases, and most importantly, effectively controlling costly chronic conditions. The easy answer to the first is that private health insurance in the U.S. is expensive. Hard-working Latinos with lower paying jobs and not offered private insurance sponsored by their employers use most if not all of their income on basic household necessities, making expensive monthly private insurance premiums to cover large families cost prohibitive. For others, private insurance is poorly understood since many are accustomed to socialized single-payer medical systems in their countries of origin.

In Mexico for example, the main medical system (called I.M.S.S.) is by law provided to all employees with both employer and employee contributing each month a fixed amount. This model has its own outpatient clinics, rural and urban general hospitals, and usually a hospital in each major city for specialists. Patients do not pay when they see a provider or have surgery. An approved, limited pharmaceutical formulary is available for free or at minimal cost, or the patient may pay out of pocket for more expensive medicines at a local pharmacy of their choice. The overall quality is fair, with mostly Mexican-trained doctors and nurses doing a phenomenal job given the available resources and limited wages. The concept of nurse practitioners and physician assistants, the so-called mid-levels, does not exist in Mexico. The I.M.S.S. clinics and hospitals also serve as the training programs for interns and residents as well as specialists.

The second public model in Mexico is called Salubridad. This is similar to the one above but it is meant for the poor who do not have an I.M.S.S. card or any private insurance coverage. It is generally free to patients, and completely government funded. Doctors and nurses in these hospitals perform daily miracles given the limited resources available to them.

These are the main two systems most U.S. immigrants from Mexico over the last 70 years have been used to and their remaining families in Mexico continue to rely on. Despite the benefits of these programs, preventive care, education on nutrition, disease-related programs, control of chronic diseases in these populations is largely lacking. Given that Mexico per capita has the highest rate of obesity and type II diabetes in the world, a life expectancy of only 75.15 years (72.12 years for males and 77.84 years for females), it is imperative for the public medical system and food industry to collaborate in order to tackle this extremely challenging situation. Interestingly, on average Mexicans in the U.S. live 6.65 more years than those living in Mexico.

This significant difference speaks to the younger, healthier immigrants while the older, sicker individuals remain in Mexico. It also exhibits the fact that the U.S. healthcare system is of superior quality to the Mexican system described above. Mexican Americans and Central Americans bring these beliefs and concepts about healthcare, lifestyle, and medical public health coverage to the U.S. Hence, it is not surprising Mexican Americans have a rate of type II diabetes of about 17%, or about double that of whites and some 8% higher than Blacks. Although there is a definitive genetic component, the fact is that as the Latino population rapidly grows in the U.S., with some 100 million projected by 2050, the number of patients with obesity and type II diabetes will likely explode and longevity will decrease on account of the resulting cardiovascular disease and various cancers.

Lastly, the concept of a private insurance with a deductible and co-insurance is both foreign and daunting for most Latin Americans, especially new arrivals. Many employers of Latino workers do not offer any benefits or do their best, with complicated insurance jargon, to dissuade the Latino employee from enrolling. Another subset of Latinos, especially younger ones and more recent arrivals to the U.S., think of health insurance as an unnecessary expense. Most honestly believe they are healthy and can treat any malady with over-the-counter strategies or the advice of a neighbor's wife or even a "curandero." In the event the individual or a family member becomes extremely ill, they often travel back to their country of origin for "free" care or simply go to a local hospital in the U.S. where they will receive "free" care.

A last factor is the lack of understanding about chronic disease management that requires multiple yearly visits with a qualified provider to actually control such diseases and prevent catastrophic events. Hence, when one considers all the above, plus the poverty level among Latinos qualifying them for Medicaid benefits and the elderly on Medicare, it is not surprising that about 38% have ended up on public health insurance programs. The current U.S. healthcare delivery model falls far short of addressing and ameliorating these factors or encouraging the insurance industry to provide more affordable products, especially to healthier young Latinos. In addition, every effort must be made to educate employed Latinos who qualify and can actually afford employer sponsored private insurance about taking advantage and enrolling in such policies, rather than remaining uninsured or relying on public coverage. Latinos can access online resources, often in Spanish, to help them navigate questions regarding the complex nuances of medical insurance. Others can just ask their doctor since practitioners often have at their disposal office managers and other assistants that can guide an individual on the best choices available to them. Human resources managers at their place of employment can readily assist individuals and families to pick the best product that meets their needs.

Federal and state policy makers must consider the wisest strategies to prevent, treat, and control the top chronic medical issues affecting Latin Americans. The current model falls short, even with the well-intended wellness provisions in the ACA. Why do I say that? According to the CDC database, the main causes of death of Latinos in the U.S. are about 25% from cardiovascular disease, 25% from various cancers, 10% from accidents, 7% from stroke, and 6% from diabetes. About 15% of Latinos have or develop mental health issues which, for the most part, remain unrecognized or untreated. In the Black population the causes of death have some parallels but also key differences. According to Statista 2020, the top causes of death in the Black population are as follows: 23.3% diseases of the heart, 20.8% malignant neoplasms, 5.9% accidents, 5.7% stroke, and 4.5% diabetes. In the black population, it is likely the higher rate of hypertension plays a major role in death from diseases of the heart, stroke, and renal disease. In Latinos, it is likely that the higher rate of type II diabetes plays a major role in death from cardiovascular disease, stroke, cancer, Alzheimer's disease (probably combined with vascular dementia), and renal disease. In addition, Latinos have a disproportionate rate of death by accidents (perhaps work related), and chronic liver disease, due alcohol consumption.

These critical statistics point to the fact that a one-size-fits-all healthcare delivery model and approach may fall short with the different minorities. If one also considers educational levels, language barriers, and specific cultural norms, Latinos may not be deriving the full benefit of the well-intended, but expensive public healthcare models. As the fastest growing minority with about 25% of the U.S population of Latin descent expected by 2050, cultural and language-appropriate healthcare solutions that specifically target the above diseases in Latinos, especially the metabolic syndrome (explained below), are essential. Thus far, the current public healthcare delivery model falls far short in preventing disease and controlling chronic conditions, hence any proposal to simply expand the status quo is likely to be insufficient and wasteful. A better model for Latinos and other minorities is paramount. What is that model?

THE CURRENT SITUATION AND COST

According to the KFF analysis of National Healthcare Expenditures (NHE), the CDC and National Center for Health Statistics, the 2020 NHEs were $4.1 trillion, or about $12,531 per person in the U.S., representing 19.7% of the GDP. The Center for Medicare and Medicaid Services (CMS) released the 2021-2030 projections for NHE. By 2027, NHE will be $5.96 trillion and by 2030 $6.8 trillion. In addition, the cost to cover the 73.5 million Medicare beneficiaries will be $1.437 trillion ($19,546 per person), and another $992.1 billion to cover 82.5 million Medicaid recipients ($12,029 per person). This illustrates that IRS tax collections will not likely suffice. Needless to say, a Medicare-for-all model may be unfathomable, especially since in 2021, the private sector pays about 50% of all NHE. Furthermore, the congressional budget office cost estimate for the ACA is $1.76 trillion for the ten-year period of 2012-2021, more expensive than initially anticipated, to eventually cover roughly 22 million individuals, costing an average of $8,000 per person. This does not include the out-of-pocket high deductibles for the most common bronze and silver insurance exchange policies sold under the ACA and the billions paid for high deductibles and increasing insurance premiums paid by consumers who stayed on their own private insurance. We currently have about thirty to thirty-five million people completely uninsured in the U.S. Just to compare, the 2019 NHE (National Healthcare Expenditures) in Canada were $264 billion (11.6% of GDP) to cover about 37.5 million people or a per capita cost of about $7,000. That is about $1,000 less per person less than the cost of the ACA to cover the entire population of Canada. It is a well-known fact that Canadians do experience significant delays for a variety of non-urgent medical, radiologic, and surgical services. Many who can afford it prefer to come to the U.S. to get such services promptly, including specialist consultations and treatments. These NHE do not include the extra expenses that will be incurred by Medicare and Medicaid services provided to the more than two million undocumented immigrants that have arrived in the last two years. Clearly, the ACA and private sector coverage models need to be remodeled with strict cost containment to truly slow down this drastic picture. The U.S. already, by far, has the most expensive NHEs than all other OECD countries. Simply applying a Medicare-for-all strategy (as some politicians have been promoting) or a public option for those over fifty years of age to purchase Medicare, will not slow down the cost avalanche, but instead dramatically increase it.

WHAT DO LATINOS NEED?

Traditionally, Latinos, especially Mexican Americans, have not trusted American doctors and the American medical system. What are the reasons for this mistrust? Aside from real language barriers, fears of discrimination, fears of excessive charges, less acculturation in more recent immigrants, historic sterilization without prior consent, is the superimposed cultural trait of many Latinos who are used to "first try self-treating" strategies since in their home countries most pharmacies do not require a provider's prescription. All too often a Latino needing medical advice, especially one without a high school diploma, first gets it from the media, doctor google, neighbor's wife, or even from a local healer. Only when all fails, begrudgingly, a trained doctor's consult and care is obtained. Then when pharmaceuticals are prescribed, these are either not filled or not taken as prescribed. So, when that individual inevitably returns to the doctors' office sicker than before, upset at having to pay again, stating the treatment did not work, it takes but a few questions to get to the bottom of the situation. More often than not, long-term compliance with the prescribed medical regimen is compromised. Some statistics show that diabetes, blood pressure, and cholesterol control, three key chronic diseases highly prevalent in minorities, especially various Latino groups, are not optimally controlled in more than 30% of individuals. This is particularly the case in patients cared for by the current public healthcare model. The concept of controllable but not curable chronic diseases such as the ones above is a bit nebulous for some Latinos. This is an important issue that requires repeated office visits during the first year of treatment, perhaps eight to twelve such interactions, with a caring provider able to clearly articulate preventive strategies and long-term treatments to achieve control of these chronic diseases in a culturally and linguistically appropriate fashion. To change an individual's lifestyle is a time-consuming task requiring health education, plenty of patience, encouragement, and genuine affirmation for each step forward the patient attains.

In spite of these matters and the increased risk of most Latinos for developing chronic diseases, they overall enjoy on average a longer life by some three years than whites and more than six years than Blacks. Why is this? No clear explanation exists but there are several viable theories. Among potential reasons are that many older Hispanics return to their country of origin to retire with family. Most Latinos, as the backbone of the current blue-collar marketplace in the U.S., are involved in manual labor jobs that demand daily energy expenditure that helps maintain healthy parameters. Unfortunately, long-standing cultural dietary and culinary customs need widespread hands-on efforts to educate populations at risk for chronic diseases that consume some 80% of the National Healthcare Expenditures (NHE). Most Latinos identify with family mealtimes as a daily essential part of their vitality and culture. These are unique to other cultures as well and should not be abandoned, but encouraged. The main issue is to consistently eat healthier and apply portion control. The approach must involve a collaborative national effort by the entire food industry, including national fast-food and soda corporations, to work with the federal and state government, medical associations, and the private sector, with the singular goal of improving the quality of affordable foods readily available to all Americans. This obviously represents an enormous task, especially when one considers the profit motive and the role of powerful lobbies. However, if significant efforts are not made to gradually improve the quality of nutrition in the U.S., which unfortunately influences the pattern of nutrition in many developing nations, the health of the nation, especially that of the socioeconomically disadvantaged, will continue down the current slippery slope. Recent strategies by politicians to regulate soda serving sizes and healthier school lunches, including no meat Fridays, have met with derision and lack of widespread appeal. We must learn from these efforts, so that future endeavors, perhaps spearheaded by the more credible medical establishment, may have a greater and durable impact on changing nutrition and activity behaviors.

While an individual has little power with bringing the above coalition together, he or she can actually dramatically improve the quality of daily foods they and their children consume. The information on healthy eating is easily found online and certainly at doctors' offices. If millions gradually change to healthier lifestyles, the food fast industry and others will get the message and eventually offer healthier products. In addition, the federal government can consider offering tax incentives to the fast-food industry companies that incorporate healthier and affordable foods on their menus. I call this The Reverse Tax Program (RTP), which rewards companies the lower the sugar and saturated fat content in their products. This would be an impressive congressional task to undertake for interested lawmakers. We have already begun to see such important changes, starting with individual behavior and accountability, but much work remains.

Another factor impacting longevity is genetics. Most Latino

groups have genetics from indigenous people that crossed the Bering Strait arguably 15,000 years ago, some gradually populating present day North America while others continued their journey all the way to the southern tip of Chile. For the most part, these were hunter-gatherer nomadic tribes who seasonally moved to fertile regions. Their diets were mostly vegan, full of nuts and various fruits, especially berries and roots, and rarely animal-based proteins. They did not develop chronic diseases, most dying from conflicts of war and accidents. The cow and the horse did not exist. No other beasts of burdens existed to help with land cultivation. Most did not enter into the era of the Agricultural Revolution that the western and northern Europeans adopted some 10,000 years ago, who gradually adapted to higher saturated fats and various sugars in their diet. This led to the development of the western diet that, when adopted by indigenous people all over the world in the 1900s, resulted in a dramatic increase in obesity, diabetes, hypertension, cholesterol elevation, gout, gallbladder disease, cardiovascular disease, and various cancers. It is not surprising that over the last 200 years (post the industrial revolution), with the ever-deteriorating quality of food that is currently affordable to most Latinos, combined with the above cultural dietary choices of daily high saturated fats and refined sugars, higher rates of western diseases would result in these Latinos not yet adapted to such insults on their metabolism.

Minimal visceral weight gain in some Latino groups, results in pre-diabetes mostly without any symptoms, then over a four-to-ten-year time span full type II Diabetes ensues, unless preventive strategies are instituted. From there it's a slippery slope with such individuals gradually developing some or most of the components known as Metabolic Syndrome, affecting approximately 25% of the entire adult U.S. population. Latinos, Native Americans, Pacific Islanders, and Native Alaskans, are on average affected at a higher rate (34% to 36%). Puerto Ricans are affected the most, then Mexican Americans. The cluster of diseases that makes up metabolic syndrome includes hypertension, pre-diabetes or full diabetes, elevated triglycerides, low HDL cholesterol and central obesity. A better name for this syndrome is Cardio-Metabolic Inflammatory Disease (CMID), since a state of vascular inflammation throughout the body causes increasing health problems, eventually overtaking most organ systems and resulting in their gradual failure.

Genetically susceptible individuals start to develop insulin resistance syndrome as visceral obesity and a sedentary lifestyle become the norm. Insulin is the hormone produced by the pancreas whose main job is to interact with receptors on a cell surface and trigger a signal to readily allow the glucose into the cell. As visceral obesity develops, a variety of inflammatory hormones are produced, preventing insulin from doing its job (insulin resistance syndrome). Over time, unless significant lifestyle modifications are embraced, type 2 diabetes occurs. In the next 10 to 20 years catastrophic cardiovascular renal and other complications inevitably ravage the patient. With proper medical assessment and lifestyle changes, the progression of insulin resistance can be slowed and even reversed. This is critical for all pre-diabetics but in particular Mexican Americans, and perhaps other Latinos as well, for reasons previously mentioned, who frequently do not seek medical attention till late in the course of their disease process. Is our current health care system helping curve this situation?

THE ACA - WHAT HAPPENED?

The architects of The Affordable Care Act (ACA) attempted to promote a bevy of great policies, including yearly wellness exams, diabetic and cancer screenings, and discounts on medications. However, as often occurs with large paradigm-shifting government programs, good intentions frequently open a Pandora's Box of seemingly unintended consequences. To begin with, the lobbyists for the American Hospital Association, big pharma, and the insurance companies played a major role in the formation and passing of the ACA along with the Obama administration. We, the doctors and patients, had little to no voice in the matter. Not surprisingly, the greatest beneficiaries from a financial standpoint from the ACA were the insurance carriers, the pharmaceutical industry, and the American Hospital institutional models. In quick time, the ACA turned the medical profession upside down, with large swaths of practitioners unable to keep viability and having to shut their offices, even many in business for more than ten years. The vast majority of primary care independent physicians experienced a significant reduction in reimbursement for their services, some up to 35%. For most specialists, reimbursement decreased from 30% to 75%, with cardiologists, who treat mostly older patients on Medicare with cardiovascular disease, the number one killer, being reduced the most. To overcome this deficit, primary care providers soon started to stay open later, see more patients, spend less time with each, offer a variety of "cash only" cosmetic procedures, and sell whatever wellness or nutritional supplements they could peddle to their patients.

This brand-new financial hardship resulted in the creation of a new cottage industry in the U.S. called ancillary testing. These businesses were mostly started by opportunists, some who had never worked in medicine, seeing the ACA's mandate on wellness testing as a perfect money-making scheme to get struggling physicians to order as many tests as possible at their new laboratory which could provide compound pharmacy products, urine toxicology, pharmacogenetics, and cancer and cardiovascular genetic screening. These ancillaries were not only expensive but, for the most part, did not benefit patient care. Providers struggling to remain viable in their private practices, having decreased their salaries by more than 50% and at times having to put the office payroll on their personal credit cards, went into a state of panic. All their best years of life devoted to studying, countless sleepless night on call during their residency at the mercy of a beeper, and the subsequent years of successful medical practices, were now all undone in a short period of time by the new ACA. This was the collateral damage brought by the ACA, with a domino effect of consequences, like a wrecking ball on the medical establishment. It appears that the lawyers and accountants responsible for shaping the ACA never asked doctors what the best way forward might be. The average consumer and public at large remained unaware of the internal financial destruction of most medical professionals. Physicians became an easy target for the attractive sales-pitch from an ancillary lab, promising "legal" payments from the enormous profits being made. The practice of medicine in the U.S. had become a Faustian ordeal. But the situation would still get worse.

In time, the billions made by the ancillary companies and participating providers would raise suspicion and federal investigators started to uncover the incestuous relationships of many such laboratories and providers. As many such enterprises were uncovered and prosecuted, most primary care providers and specialists distanced themselves from such schemes, and those that had not participated and continued to experience financial hardship, rushed in large numbers, literally on their knees, to hospitals for a guaranteed salary. The sweetheart deal obtained by the lobbyists on behalf of the American Hospital Association allowed hospitals to rapidly become not-for-profit entities in large numbers and to "acquire" distressed primary care and specialist practices and place such practitioners on quota driven compensation packages. To maintain good standing, it was necessary to refer specific patients for high reimbursement procedures such as spine surgery and other orthopedic interventions, cardiovascular testing, all kinds of invasive interventions, cardiac surgery, device placement, neurosurgical treatments, weight loss procedures, MRIs, and to the hospital's own ancillary laboratory. Obviously, patients covered by the best commercial insurance plans were targeted and Medicare patients were also signaled out. Medicaid and Obamacare covered patients were shunned since these policies did not reimburse enough. In addition, consumers that continued to purchase private insurance policies saw their monthly premiums rise by several hundred percent over the next five years. Many individuals shifted to high deductible policies, which caused large numbers not to see a doctor when needed out of fear of having to cover the deductible out of pocket. This model persists and has caused escalating costs and the erosion of the patient-provider relationship. Billing under a hospital's tax identification number automatically gets paid at a higher rate than an independent provider for the same procedure and service. Independent doctors gradually driven out of business have had to see a patient every ten minutes non-stop all day, retire, or accept the Faustian contract. In 2018 a Harvard-trained, early-sixties, interventional cardiologist acquaintance of mine told me he was one of the fortunate ones in his group. When I asked for the details, he confessed that his wife was partner in a law firm, so with grown children out of the house he had become a hypnotist at a private prep-school. He had been able to teach the girls cross country team members who to push through the pain of running to earn a state championship. Bravo for the ACA! I wonder if a hypnotist ever became a practicing cardiologist. Probably not. Perhaps in the not-too-distant future a cardiologist will be asked by Congress to gather some of his medical friends, maybe some accountants, and even though none have any experience in the law, be given the task to change the expensive, convoluted legal profession to cut hourly rates and make it more affordable, especially to minorities and the poor. I am not holding my breath on this one!

The sad part for the consumer is that the era of the independent country doctor, the trusted family practitioner, and bias-free second opinions are for the most part a thing of the past. Institutional corporate medicine has become a behemoth that seeks regional monopolistic tactics in each market, with rapidly growing administrative positions often paid higher than the doctors, further distancing themselves from the actual daily needs of the community. These models do not seek to care for patients on Obamacare insurance plans since they know patients have extremely high deductibles and reimbursement is low. In the outpatient setting, patients with Medicaid policies and Obamacare insurance have an extremely difficult time finding primary care providers and find securing a consult with a specialist almost impossible. The reimbursement from such policies and Medicaid products is extremely low such that most providers who see many of these patients struggle financially to pay the overhead and keep the door open. The government has not made it any easier on independent physicians and so many have simply retired. The myriad of franchise taxes, pay roll taxes, sales taxes, state taxes, malpractice insurance, umbrella insurance, rent, cost of supplies, license fees, continuing medical operation, technology costs, equipment leases, electronic health acre record costs, and employee payroll, all choke the primary care provider to the point of exhaustion, depression, and non-viability.

All of these changes in the medical field impact the majority of patients, with the exception of those who can afford medical care out of pocket, but those living in poverty are affected the most. Minorities and others on public insurance suffer the most in this scenario, with little actual time spent with a doctor, now gradually replaced by mid-level practitioners. When a provider has to see five or six patients an hour to barely make payroll, little to no time is given to preventive medical care or control of chronic diseases. Illnesses and diseases will ultimately cost the healthcare system far more, especially in those afflicted with the metabolic syndrome, since the catastrophic heart attack, stroke, congestive heart failure, or renal failure will one day occur, unless effective care is started on a timely fashion and adhered to over time. In order to control these chronic diseases that end up taking up some 80% of all healthcare expenditures, providers must connect with patients to build trust. This takes time and multiple visits, perhaps ten to twelve in the first year alone, especially with various minorities, such as the Latinos, each with their own cultural nuances.

The current model is failing simply because it prevents the above close-knit, trusting connection from becoming cemented and the time-consuming task of educating and keeping the patient accountable. Only then will the patient experience better health and optimal outcomes. Then the work continues with the on-going communication and discipline required in the maintenance phase. It is the only way to continue to educate, especially about lifestyle choices, including the dangers of the fast-food industry, convenience stores, and soda consumption so ingrained in the Latino daily routine, especially in Mexican Americans. Then there are also the pervasive alcohol and tobacco abuse. Furthermore, the basics of grocery shopping for affordable healthy foods, understanding nutrition labels, and promoting the avoidance of sugary and fatty options are essential components of the education about disease in the Latino population. These interactions at times are far more effective in the culturally appropriate language of their country of origin.

The clear point is that certain people, especially Latinos for all the reasons described above, require a constant medical guardian angel to reach and maintain optimal health. One must understand and respect that their religious faith, especially for older individuals, is of critical importance to the emotional and physical wellbeing of the patient. Currently, far less than 50% of Latinos in the present medical public health model are able to maintain control of their particular chronic diseases, let alone prevent them. The concept of primordial prevention, that is educating parents to prevent the risk factors from emerging in their children, is a foreign concept in most medical primary care offices. Maternal nutrition, especially in Latino mothers-to-be, is a critical factor in preventing the future development of type II diabetes and other metabolic syndrome components in her offspring, especially at a young age. This is a generational matter, with future generations developing diabetes at a younger and younger age. Unfortunately, not even a top hypnotist or a magician can achieve such patient evaluations, prevention, treatment, and control of chronic disease with effective outcomes in ten-to-fifteen-minute office visits every three to four months, as the current healthcare delivery model permits.

Or should the provider give up and call Faust for the hospital employment contract? The fact is that we will be experiencing a 100,000-140,000-physician shortage by 2030 (MDs). Will this deficit be filled with mid-level providers such as nurse practitioners and physician assistants? Or perhaps by bringing foreign-trained physicians? This is not like the current manual labor force where low income, low salaried manual laborers (the Latinos) can be indiscriminately shuffled in to fill a spot. Can the medical profession recover a prior time of strong patient-physician relationships, financial viability and independent decision making? Can the era of good treatments incorporate an effective, high quality, and affordable preventive model early in life? Would it be ideal for groups of providers to branch out and focus on the comprehensive prevention and management of metabolic syndrome patients, especially in minorities most afflicted?

It is evident that cost containment strategies are essential for any healthcare delivery model to serve the individual and communities. This includes independent medical decision making by providers that are not beholden to hospital institutions for quota-driven compensation packages as some 70-80% of doctors find themselves tied to. Other providers are independent in their practices but have billing and collection hospital/institutional-based contracts that allow them to obtain higher reimbursement for office medical services, yet commit them to refer to that parent institution for specialist consults, ambulatory, and in-hospital procedures and surgeries. The concern on a "Medicare-for-all" proposed model by politicians is that since Medicare reimburses hospitals on average some 40% less than private insurance payers, the volume of testing and surgeries will only rise in compensation. We have seen this already in the ACA era. This resulted in an escalating price war with skyrocketing insurance premiums, higher deductibles, and outrageous hospital charges. The tax-paying consumer, mostly the middle class, has borne the brunt of this phenomenon. Already in the U.S., we are performing far more surgeries per 100,000 people than all other western countries with similar socioeconomic status and, with few exceptions, no better outcomes.

Before I provide a proposal for a healthcare delivery model for the U.S. in the addendum that follows this narrative, let me first briefly return to diabetes and the metabolic syndrome so critical for the health of Latinos.

THE DIABETES AND METABOLIC SYNDROME SLIPPERY SLOPE

Once pre-diabetes has been present for some four to five years, the conversion rate to full diabetes is 25% per year. By this time, the overworked pancreas has struggled for too long, trying to overproduce insulin, such that 80% of the cells that produce insulin are no longer functional. No matter how much insulin is produced, the receptors on the cell are prevented from locking up the insulin, hence blood glucose levels elevate. At first the patient does not experience any symptoms but damage has already begun. The microscopic changes and disfunction occurring mean the brain, heart, kidney, liver, and other organs do not receive the optimal blood flow with its nutrients and oxygen, or the ability to take away toxic waste products. These processes are essential and the impact high blood glucose has on pretty much every part of the body is what makes diabetes so dangerous. That, and the fact that these things are occurring ten, fifteen, twenty years before an individual is diagnosed. Eventually vascular dementia develops, with the expected mild to moderate or even severe cognitive impairment. This scenario is different than Alzheimer's disease but in many such patients it co-exists. Some have even called vascular dementia as type III diabetes. About a third of all cases of dementia can be prevented by initially detecting those most at risk, effectively treating, and controlling the above metabolic syndrome diseases. I hope you'll give me grace for this seemingly rabbit trail. However, with the rates of obesity and type II diabetes in the Latino population, this issue is intrinsically linked to overall Latino health and abundant living.

HONDA TO BMW

So, how do we accomplish effective prevention and treatment with nearly 100 million adults, many of them Latinos, in the U.S. who need metabolic syndrome education, prevention, management, or control? It is imperative that we in the healthcare sector focus on helping such patients gain control over their lives and prevent the development of the syndrome or any of its individual components in those not yet afflicted.

All too often I have heard the typical list of grievances about the expensive doctor that hardly spent time with a patient, prescribed medications that didn't cure their problems so they stopped taking them and quickly feels poorly again with high blood sugar, high blood pressure, and no significant changes the lifestyle. I say to these individuals, "I need to change you from a HONDA to a BMW." A blank look typically ensues. Not an automobile issue, I assure them. Then I reveal they are a "Hypertensive Obese Non-compliant Diabetic Adult" (a HONDA) that needs tremendous medical care and committed lifestyle change to reach an optimal health status I like to call "Best Metabolic Wellness" (BMW). So, they need to transform a HONDA to a BMW! This is actually an essential outpatient clinic preventive strategy, and chronic disease management goals for the 34% to 36% of the Latino population. A must for any effective present and future healthcare delivery model in the U.S.

PUBLIC HEALTH AND LATINOS

Healthcare is a key political issue with Latinos, since so many depend on Medicaid and Medicare. The obvious main reasons are that private health insurance is expensive, especially in covering larger families, many are employed in businesses that do not offer such coverage, and others have limited household income level, qualifying them for enrollment in Medicaid.

More dependence on public health is not necessarily the answer, though. If the goal is to prevent disease and control chronic diseases, a better delivery model is essential. Part of this model involves educating Latinos on being more proactive about disease prevention and becoming more informed on their particular maladies. Latinos traditionally have not participated in such activities and not uncommonly have little knowledge about medicine and health, with large numbers relying on misinformation from a neighbor, television ads, online, or gossip magazines. Interestingly, Latinos tend to participate in community activities at varying rates. Only 30-40% of

Latino parents involve themselves in their children's schools, 40% in charitable organizations, 70% in their local church, and less than 10% participate in protests, lobbying, working in political campaigns, political rallies, or in seeking policy making influence.

Higher involvement in all the above community activities is extremely important, as well as involvement in activities that educate families about health and medicine. Churches, community centers, and schools could provide, free of charge, education and accurate information on medicine and specific diseases afflicting Latino populations, especially on the metabolic syndrome. However, the ideal situation is for Latinos at risk for metabolic syndrome and other chronic conditions, to have a close, trusting, and frequent contact type of relationship with their doctors. As the population of Latinos grows to 100 million within the next few decades, an alternate, more efficient, affordable, and high-quality healthcare model than the current public system will be essential. Without that, people, especially Latinos, will continue to get sicker at younger ages with chronic diseases and as a nation we will experience by 2030 the already prognosticated $6 trillion a year invoice.

There are many of us in healthcare who are fully aware of the waste and excesses in our present model. In his 2019 book titled *The Price We Pay*, Dr. Marty Makary describes in detail "What Broke American Health Care – And How to Fix It." He identifies multiple areas of abuse and where significant cost-containment may be obtained without compromising quality. To that effect, I have proposed an alternate model called The Blended Plan, A Medicare Optional Model. This incorporates many of the suggestions made by

Dr. Makary and his team at Johns Hopkins, and emphasizes the medical home primary care component affordably available to all citizens and residents. In addition, the model includes a commercial insurance-sponsored program, income dependent, for all hospital and specialty services. It provides options for young individuals currently without any coverage and for those under 65 years of age to opt into it. Some OECD nations have been employing similar formats successfully. The entire model may be tested in a pilot study prior to more widespread implementation. It promises to save some 30% on NHEs! I do realize this is a lofty goal, some may say an impossible dream, but we need answers, sooner than later.

CONCLUSIONS

Do Mexicans matter? Whatever your opinion may be on this question, my hope is that this narrative has provided insight into the history of Mexican Americans throughout the different eras, from the Spanish-Mexico period through the post Mexican-American War years and to the modern age. My interest has not been in providing revisionist history with the intent of embellishing a victimhood status, so common in modern times, but sticking to the truth of how actual events occurred, no matter how prejudicial and abhorrent against Mexicans, and the significant social, legal, and political advances that the U.S. has achieved, especially since the mid-1960s. The current heated dialogue on race, ethnicity, and skin color in our society has for the most part been seen by the mainstream media, politicians, and the public at large in the U.S. as a Black-white binary problem, for the most part ignoring Latinos and other minorities. Hence, we Latinos at times feel like a forgotten, taken-for-granted minority. In essence, "The Other Minority," important only for the manual labor we provide, especially in agriculture, the service industry, the military, and construction. However, I honestly believe that this young country, still sanctifying Jefferson's "all men are created equal" statement in the Declaration of Independence, as some of the mightiest words ever written in the English language, but not actually applying the concept from onset in the day-to-day experience, to the detriment of most minorities and women, has in recent times elevated its collective conscience, in ethical, practical, and philosophical constructs, such that now we may truly live by those exalted words to the benefit of us all. The ideal also included in this statement, as Frederick Douglass predicted, has led to a new post-racism, post-discrimination era that we should all embrace as progress, and as an amazing accomplishment of the U.S.

I do not think we who are minorities need to identify ourselves any longer by the color of our skin, our race, or ethnicity as the primary characteristics that define who we are. These aspects of our being are a part of who we are and sometimes impact our lives, but are not the end all and be all of our identity. We need not accept handouts or positions principally because of these qualities instead of our very real talent and merit earned through dedication, commitment, perseverance, education, and, lastly, plain hard work. Political positions mainly filled on a quota system based on gender, skin color, and ethnicity, instead of who can actually do the job based on their

> Skin color, race, or are part of who we are and sometimes impact our lives, but are not the end all and be all of our identity.

education, experience, and demonstrable track record, does a disservice to everyone.

When someone asks me to describe myself, this is what I say: I'm a loving father of four young adults, all university graduates or currently attaining higher education, a person who had the privilege to take advantage of educational opportunities to serve my community as a double medical specialist, someone who loves to read, travel, watch historical movies, stay in healthy shape, and converse with anyone and everyone, especially if they possess a glittering, sparkling mind and a keen sense of humor, for daily laughter is essential. The word Hispanic or Latino does not come out of my mouth when I describe myself, but "I'm an American" does. I sometimes say I've had the opportunity to live in both Canada and Mexico for prolonged periods of time. You may not believe me when I tell you I did not readily know that I was Hispanic or Latino or whatever you may want to define me as, until well into my mid-to late-30s. In my 30 plus years in the U.S., as a first generation Mexican American, I have not experienced any racism, discrimination, or denial of opportunity. I have not seen any form of institutional racism, especially the types so prevalent in the first two eras of this narrative. I have experienced total acceptance and inclusivity by all the amazing people I've had the privilege to meet in the U.S. As a doctor, I have achieved the "American Dream." No one stood in my way, for I have had every opportunity a country can offer a newcomer, never denied or purposely derailed. When I have not done well, say in a business venture or investment, it's not been on account of racism of any kind, it's usually been entirely my fault. If the mainstream media or current politicians want to portray some sort of victimhood status for me due to my brown skin and being a minority, please do not, for it is not the truth. Advancing such narratives harms minorities who are unfortunately made to believe that someone else is responsible for their difficult situation, that they are not capable or talented enough to overcome adversities and attain success, and must rely on big government to solve their problems. This type of messages creates generational dependency and sabotages the ability of minorities to break this sick cycle that results in perpetual poverty and heart break.

Now again, I don't want to imply that no one in America experiences racism or discrimination. But when they do, there are ways to respond that brings them down to the level of the ignorant, hateful person and there are ways to respond that lifts them up and promotes healing, happiness, and contentment. I choose the latter and encourage every other minority to do the same. There's a saying that goes like this: You can't be a victim and victorious at the same time. Let's choose victory.

The challenge to Latinos, who tend to be easy-going and willing to work hard under almost any circumstance, is to not depend on government, not to become an underclass, valued only for manual labor, but instead to ascend by taking advantage of the myriad of opportunities this amazing country has to offer. I have no doubt we Latinos, with our talent, joy of life, diligence, and industriousness, all smartly applied, will continue to achieve the highest levels in U.S. society, including politics. Perhaps one can say the "American Dream" during the second era discussed in this book, from 1848 to

1968, was achieved, at least in part, at the expense of Mexicans. But now, in this the twenty-first century, this same "American Dream" paradigm can be achieved in the U.S. because of contributions of Mexican Americans (and other Latinos). To that effect, this "Other Minority" should not be dismissed or taken for granted, but given its rightful place in U.S. society, appreciated for its many past and present contributions, and its diverse cultures, all undoubtedly contributing, and creating in the coming hundred years an even better, and more unified United States of America. I even dream of a day when a talented, conscientious individual of Mexican descent, with great accomplishments and of superb capabilities, man or woman, is elected President of the U.S. based on these qualities, not their skin color or gender.

Epilogue – My Immigration Story & Final Thoughts

What many fail to understand is that the personal value of U.S. citizenship is incalculable. That is how I felt in 2007 when I finally became a U.S. citizen and how I still feel today. When I initially arrived in the U.S. for medical residency training in June 1990, I did so with a J-1 visa. It was clearly stipulated that once I completed the residency and fellowship sub-specialty training, the visa would expire and I had to leave the country within 6 months. By the end of 1996 I had completed both Internal Medicine and Cardiology programs at Baylor College of Medicine in Houston, Texas. My plan was to move back to Mexico and open a practice in Cancún. I was married with three young children. My wife at the time, born in Alexandria, Virginia, became apprehensive about an imminent move to a beach resort in Mexico. Unfortunately, since early 1994 Mexico had sustained increasing instability on account of the Zapatista uprising, multiple political and drug cartel related murders, various corruption scandals, prolific kidnapping rings and to top it off, more currency devaluations. It was simply not the best time to make a major family move to unstable and potentially dangerous circumstances. But what were our options?

When I inquired with immigration officials, I was unceremoniously informed that the U.S. had no use for someone like me. That is, an educated, bilingual individual with a premedical training from the University of Toronto and the University of Western Ontario, a medical degree from the Universidad de Monterrey and two medical specialty degrees in Internal Medicine and Cardiology! I had six months to leave or I would be in violation of the terms of my J-1 visa. The fact that in 1997 I was married to a U.S. citizen and had three children, all three years of age and under, including a newborn, was not sufficient for me to be granted a work visa, green card, a pathway to residency, or any other way to stay in the U.S.

Voicing my despair, a colleague at the hospital introduced me to the J-1 visa waiver program that had been set up in order to bring well-trained doctors to areas and counties of medical necessity where U.S. citizen doctors did not want to go. In order to obtain such a waiver, I would have to advertise in various periodicals for at least six months for a position in primary care and only when no qualified

U.S. citizen doctor applied for the job, then I cloud be awarded the waiver. Lastly, it was a three-year commitment and then I would be awarded a green card. Through a series of convoluted events, prior to the information being available on a google search, I was fortunate to locate an opportunity in Dangerfield, Texas, in Morris County, a medically underserved community with a large African American population. A great group out of a premier facility, Trinity Mother Francis Hospital in Tyler, Texas, was prepared to hire me on the condition that I would be expanding their brand in that area, including Mt. Pleasant, Texas, some 90 miles north of Tyler. As I mentioned previously, Harold Nix, a Texas tobacco attorney helped me enormously with the visa waiver. When the J-1 visa waiver was finally granted, I moved the family to our brand-new house and I was eager and ready to go to work. At the end of 1999, as promised, I received a precious green card in the mail.

Once we relocated to Dallas, Texas, I initially joined a cardiology group and within six months I decided it would be best to open my own practice. I did so in a small community called Ferris, Texas, south of Dallas in Ellis County. I immediately felt right at home, welcomed with open arms by Dr. Robert Megna, a primary care physician in that town, in similar fashion as in my East Texas experiences. My family thrived in our new Dallas environment. Eventually I got around to applying for U.S. citizenship, which was granted to me in 2007 in a beautiful ceremony along with thousands of others from all over the world. It had merely taken seventeen years, but no matter the journey, the value of U.S. citizenship is incalculable.

Will those crossing the border on this very day, granted all kinds of liberties, freedoms, and privileges, eventually truly feel the same love an appreciation for the U.S. that I have felt all these years in my heart? Can someone that brashly violates another country's laws ever feel that they truly earned the right and privilege to one day become a U.S. resident and citizen? Is it fair to the millions of immigrants from all over the world seeking to come to the U.S., perhaps looking for the "American Dream," applying via legal avenues, to be displaced by the millions who have crossed the border illegally over the last two years? How about those of us who went through the legal channels and waited our turn while contributing to the well-being of the country? I ask, is this open border fair to us and our families?

As one of millions of Mexican Americans currently working and contributing to the betterment and prosperity of the U.S., I can safely say that by far we want the immigration process to be legal, expeditious, and transparent. For the many that have been in the U.S. undocumented, for years working, contributing, and without any significant criminal record, there should be a straightforward and prompt immigration mechanism with a pathway to residency and citizenship that does not put the fear of deportation front and center, while allowing families to remain together. Many may prefer a simple work visa that permits them to go back and forth at their convenience to visit family and friends south of the border.

We Mexican Americans and other Latinos need to insist on the immediate implementation of a bi-partisan comprehensive plan that addresses the current open border crisis and provides ample and fair legal immigration pathways. Interestingly, in the period 2010 to

2019, the number of Mexican born individuals living in the U.S. declined by about 780,000 due in part to stricter immigration policies and a better Mexican economy, especially during the Great Recession. In recent years the number of Mexicans leaving the U.S. has been greater than new arrivals into the U.S. In fact, since 2013, Mexico is no longer the origin country of most recent immigrants, outnumbered by China and India. Unauthorized immigrants from Mexico have also been declining in numbers. However, Mexicans in the U.S. are more likely than other immigrants to be longtime residents with about 60% having arrived more than twenty years ago, resulting in large numbers remaining undocumented and marginalized in poverty, more often than not without healthcare and other benefits. There is an immediate need, as mentioned above, to bring these millions in from the cold.

The cultural and religious legacy from the Spanish conquest of Mexico to present times can be best defined as a conservative way of life. For most Mexicans, this way of life remains. Mexicans for the most part believe in God and hold tightly to traditional Christian and Catholic values. The family is at the core of their daily existence. The family is everything, all too often young children living in the same household with the parents and grandparents. This precious love of family togetherness and connectivity instinctively makes Mexicans very protective of their family's safety. The current dangerous inner-city environment and neighborhoods, so prevalent in so many large cities in the U.S., mostly on account of illegal drugs and firearms, coupled with recent policies that do not prosecute but instead put criminals back on the streets, is not supported by most Mexicans in the U.S. Recent trends to defund the police are completely unacceptable to traditional family values-oriented Mexicans.

Traditional marriages between a man and woman are simply unions blessed by God, while other concepts are respected but poorly understood and even less embraced. Abortion is an extremely difficult topic for traditional Mexicans. But the fact is that there are large numbers in the pro-choice camp as there are pro-life Mexicans. It is my personal belief that those that are pro-choice believe abortion should be legal, safe, and rare.

Work ethic is a virtuous trait in Mexicans. It has always been thus, Hollywood stereotypes notwithstanding. Just ask any passerby on a typical 105-degree humid summer day in Dallas, at about three in the afternoon, what is the likely ethnicity of the construction workers? Mexicans, young and old. It's Mexicans and more Mexicans. The current backbone of arduous physical labor in the U.S. is Mexicans. Rarely will we see other groups performing these tasks across different industries. It would not be too outlandish if I were to claim that a day, a week or a month without the Mexican workforce and ingenuity, would result in complete paralysis of the U.S. economy.

For politicians wanting to attract Mexican American votes, please consider the above paragraphs, for it is not complicated what Mexicans in the U.S. want. If you respect their traditional values, all will be well.

For the average person — the voter — whether Latino, Anglo, Black, Asian, or of other descent, I hope you're encouraged by what you've read here. My goal is to share the rich, if often tragic, history of Mexican Americans, highlighting both times of atrocity and times of great growth and improvement. While our country has come a long way, we still have many improvements we can make to benefit all American citizens. None of us can do it all, but all of us can do something. That something may be organizing information gatherings in your community or church with a doctor, nonprofit group, or speaker. It may be sharing this book with friends and family. It definitely includes voting. What a privilege we have in this country to voice our opinions and take part in who holds leadership roles! We are truly blessed to live in the United States of America. Let's not squander that blessing, but use it to better the lives of those around us in whatever way we can.

> None of us can do it all, but all of us can do something.

Dr. Federico Maese